CHURCHILL

CHURCHILL

THE PROPHETIC STATESMAN

JAMES C. HUMES

REGNERY
HISTORY

Cataloging-in-Publication data on file with the Library of Congress

ISBN 978-1-59698-775-3

Published in the United States by
Regnery History
An imprint of Regnery Publishing, Inc.
One Massachusetts Avenue NW
Washington, DC 20001
www.RegneryHistory.com

Manufactured in the United States of America

10 9 8 7 6 5 4 3 2 1

Books are available in quantity for promotional or premium use. Write to Director of Special Sales, Regnery Publishing, Inc., One Massachusetts Avenue NW, Washington, DC 20001, for information on discounts and terms, or call (202) 216-0600.

Distributed to the trade by
Perseus Distribution
250 West 57th Street
New York, NY 10107

To my daughter, Mary Humes Quillen,
without whose encouragement and urging
this book would never have been written.

CONTENTS

PART VI: THE COLD WAR

FOREWORD

BY DAVID EISENHOWER

Perhaps it is a cliché that a politician thinks of the next election and a statesman of the next generation, yet my grandfather found merit in the maxim. He had known leaders he esteemed as the greatest of statesmen: President de Gaulle, General George Marshall, Chancellor Konrad Adenauer. He also was well acquainted with the decision-making of Presidents Roosevelt and Truman. Churchill, however, was the leader he admired above all. My grandfather once said Churchill would tell his countrymen not what they wanted to hear, but what they should hear. Winston Churchill had the mind of an historian and the courage of a soldier; he would say what he thought even if he risked political death or defeat. And he had the uncanny ability to look well into the future.

In the 1930s the British people, still reeling from the massive death count and trauma of World War I, closed their ears to Churchill's warnings about the Nazis and the threat of another war. A decade later, just after World War II ended, the British could not accept the idea that their former ally, the Soviet Union, posed another threat to world peace. Then, in the 1950s, Churchill enraged Europeans—who had suffered country-destroying devastation at the hands of Hitler's Nazis—by insisting that Germany must be welcomed back into Europe's fold if the continent was to recover economically. He was jeered and attacked for this courageous and far-sighted view.

James Humes's fascinating book begins with Churchill's schoolboy essay at Harrow in which he predicts a world war beginning in 1914 marked by trench warfare and astronomical casualties. Churchill's last admonition came in an address to the American Bar Association, meeting in London in 1957, following the Soviet invasion of Hungary. He warned that the United Nations was becoming a feckless organization dominated by dictators. The free nations, in other words, would have to look within themselves to find the wisdom and resolve to navigate freedom's future challenges.

One of Churchill's most striking predictions dates from 1922 and is hauntingly relevant to the world we live in today—the probability that a fanatical Islamic sect like al Qaeda would create violence and havoc in the West.

Humes also includes in his catalogue Churchill's one notable prophetic stumble. He failed to anticipate the relatively speedy success of Overlord, the Allied landings at Normandy, and how long it would take Eisenhower's forces to reach Paris. Maybe Churchill's crystal ball was not as accurate in the short term as it was in the long term. Or maybe it became slightly cloudy when contemplating the outcome of a military campaign on which the hopes of all humanity depended, a campaign that Churchill had had the foresight to insist upon and to bring about.

In hundreds of studies of Churchill, no one else, remarkably enough, has focused on Churchill's predictions and prophecies. James Humes has produced a book that is unique as well as necessary for an understanding of statesmanship. After all, as Lincoln said in 1858, "If we could first know where we are, and whither we are tending, we could better judge what to do, and how to do it."

For anyone who wants to know how a statesman's mind works, I commend this book and the subject of Churchill.

INTRODUCTION

CHURCHILL AS PROPHET

*"There's only one political leader in history
who had his own crystal ball."*

—RICHARD NIXON ON CHURCHILL,
TO THE AUTHOR IN 1992

Winston Churchill is rightly celebrated as the greatest statesman of the twentieth century and among the greatest of
any century. His oratory rallied the British nation in its
darkest hour against fearsome odds. His grim yet inspiring acknowl-
edgment when he became prime minister that he had "nothing to offer
but blood, toil, tears, and sweat," his vow that Britain "shall fight on
the beaches," and his praise of the RAF pilots in the Battle of Britain—"Never in the field of human conflict was so much owed by so
many to so few"—will be recalled as long as men contemplate the
peaks of human eloquence.

One of the most revealing examples of his combination of prophetic vision, resoluteness, and soul-stirring oratory occurred out of
the public eye at a crucial moment early in the Second World War.

Though scarcely anyone realized it, Churchill's premiership, and with it the entire fight against Hitler, almost ended three weeks after he took office in May 1940. While Churchill was desperately trying to rally the nation and coordinate the evacuation of the trapped British Expeditionary Force from Dunkirk, a few of his government's senior members, still in the demoralizing grip of appeasement, were trying to open a back channel to Hitler to seek peace terms. Italy, not yet a belligerent, was willing to act as an intermediary. The foreign minister, Lord Halifax, was pressing hard for negotiations, and was winning some support in the small war cabinet. Churchill risked isolating himself in the fragile new government. He knew that if he sought peace terms the government, at the very least, would fall, and the consequences might indeed be much more dire. In a meeting of the war cabinet on May 28, Churchill's eighteenth day in office, he argued that "nations which went down fighting rose again, but those which surrendered tamely were finished." Halifax would not yield, however, and the argument between the two grew heated. Churchill moved to adjourn the war cabinet so that he could discuss the matter with the full cabinet.

"There now occurred one of the most extraordinary scenes of the war," Sir Martin Gilbert wrote in his official biography of Churchill. The prime minister summoned his full dramatic powers and gave one of the most forceful speeches of his life—to an audience of only forty people around the long cabinet table in 10 Downing Street. Churchill described the gloomy scene in France, anticipating that Hitler would take Paris and "offer terms" to Britain. There was no doubt, though, "that we must decline and fight on."

Hugh Dalton, the minister for economic warfare, recorded the scene in his diary:

> And then he said, "I have thought carefully in these last days whether it was part of my duty to consider entering into negotiations with That Man." But it was idle to think

that, if we tried to make peace now, we should get better terms than if we fought it out. The Germans would demand our fleet—that would be called "disarmament"—our naval bases, and much else. We should become a slave state, though a British Government which would be Hitler's puppet would be set up....

"And I am convinced," he concluded, "that every man of you would rise up and tear me down from my place if I were for one moment to contemplate parley or surrender. *If this long island story of ours is to end at last, let it end only when each one of us lies choking in his own blood upon the ground.*" [Emphasis added.]

"Not much more was said," Dalton's diary entry continues. "No one expressed even the faintest flicker of dissent." Halifax's last spasm of appeasement was dead, never to return.

Dalton's dramatic account did not surface until many years after the war. Churchill deliberately concealed this entire episode, including the climax of May 28, in his World War II memoirs out of tactful consideration for Halifax and others. He merely recorded that he gave a status report on the deteriorating conditions and insisted that, whatever happened, "we shall fight on." No mention of calling upon his colleagues to choke in their own blood, or of the bitter struggle with the last vestiges of appeasement inside his own war cabinet during the previous few days.

But the next paragraph of Churchill's recollection clearly hints that something more dramatic had taken place:

There occurred a demonstration which, considering the character of the gathering—twenty-five experienced politicians and Parliament men, who represented all the different points of view, whether right or wrong, before the war—surprised me. Quite a number seemed to jump up from the

table and come running to my chair, shouting and patting
me on the back. There is no doubt that had I at this junc-
ture faltered at all in the leading of the nation, I should have
been hurled out of office.

Left unsaid is that had Churchill yielded to the last gasp of the appeasers, it surely would have resulted in Hitler's complete triumph in
Europe. Churchill understood that this would be the end not only of
the war but of Western civilization itself. If Hitler wins, he warned,
"then the whole world, including the United States, including all that
we have known and care for, will sink into the abyss of a new Dark
Age, made more sinister, and perhaps more protracted, by the lights
of perverted science."

Could anyone have predicted that Britain would ever find itself in
such a desperate situation, and that it would require the supreme
character of someone like Churchill to survive the storm, who would
tell the world that Britain would *never surrender*? Actually, someone
did predict it, almost forty years before. And that person was Winston
Churchill himself.

———◆———

Cast your mind for a moment back to 1898. Churchill, a young
officer in General Sir Herbert Kitchener's army, participated in what
is said to have been the last cavalry charge in British history[1], against
the lines of the "Dervishes" of the Mahdist army in Khartoum. The
British had sent Kitchener's expeditionary force to the Sudan to avenge
the death of General Charles Gordon at the hands of the Mahdi—
Mohammed Ahmed—and shore up the exposed southern flank of
Egypt. It was a long and arduous campaign, but the superiority of
British arms left no doubt about the outcome. The ultimate battle was
a one-sided slaughter, giving Churchill his first glimpse of the horror

of modern warfare soon to visit the twentieth century on a vast scale. He wrote an extensive account of the campaign in one of his early books, *The River War*.

It is clear from Churchill's account that he understood that what he called "the terrible machinery of scientific war" would mark a turning point in human affairs in the twentieth century, with the most profound implications for soldiers and their commanders, civilian statesmen, and general populations alike. His experience in the Sudan campaign was the basis for much of his foresight into the social and political trends in the twentieth century and even today.

Churchill's narration of the climactic battle of Omdurman captures well the scale of the raw slaughter of modern warfare:

> [M]ore than 12,000 [British] infantry were engaged in that mechanical scattering of death which the polite nations of the earth have brought to such monstrous perfection.... They fired steadily and stolidly, without hurry or excitement, for the enemy were far away and the officers careful. Besides, the soldiers were interested in the work and took great pains. But presently the mere physical act became tedious. The tiny figures seen over the slide of the backsight seemed a little larger, but also fewer at each successive volley. The rifles grew hot—so hot that they had to be changed for those of the reserve companies. The Maxim guns exhausted all the water in their jackets, and several had to be refreshed from the water-bottles of the Cameron Highlanders before they could go on with their deadly work. The empty cartridge-cases, tinkling to the ground, formed small but growing heaps beside each man. And all the time out on the plain on the other side bullets were shearing through flesh, smashing and splintering bone; blood spouted from terrible wounds; valiant men were struggling on through a hell of whistling metal, exploding

shells, and spurting dust—suffering, despairing, dying. Such was the first phase of the battle of Omdurman.

The Khalifa's plan of attack appears to have been complex and ingenious. It was, however, based on an extraordinary miscalculation of the power of modern weapons; with the exception of this cardinal error, it is not necessary to criticise it.

Nearly ten thousand Dervishes were killed in this attack, an equal number wounded. British casualties were few in what has been called more an execution than a battle.

But Churchill does not leave the matter there. One of the mistaken clichés about Churchill is that he was a racist imperialist. (Is there any other kind in the annals of modern political correctness?) If this were true, his account in *The River War* would be a Manichean tale of the complete triumph of the superior forces of good over the forces of evil and depravity. He might have been expected to evince the attitude of Hilaire Belloc's lyric,

Whatever happens, we have got
The Maxim Gun, and they have not.

Yet *The River War* betrays no European insolence. Although Churchill had some bracing criticisms of Islam, as we shall see later, *The River War* is remarkable for its consideration of the courage, virtue, and humanity of the enemy. It includes stiff criticism of the conduct of the British military. (Indeed, this is one reason Churchill later suppressed the first edition of *The River War*, which threatened to become an embarrassment to his early political career, and hastily republished a heavily abridged edition.) It is an account that the academic critic would call "fair-minded."

Churchill offered sympathy and praise for the vanquished foe, culminating in a remarkable lesson that he hoped readers would take from the scene:

> Yet these were as brave men as ever walked the earth. The conviction was borne in on me that their claim beyond the grave in respect of a valiant death was not less good than that which any of our countrymen could make.... The valour of their deed has been discounted by those who have told the tale. "Mad fanaticism" is the depreciating comment of their conquerors. I hold this to be a cruel injustice. Nor can he be a very brave man who will not credit them with a nobler motive, and believe that they died to clear their honour from the stain of defeat. Why should we regard as madness in the savage what would be sublime in civilised men?
>
> *For I hope that if evil days should come upon our own country, and the last army which a collapsing Empire could interpose between London and the invader were dissolving in rout and ruin, that there would be some—even in these modern days—who would not care to accustom them-selves to a new order of things and tamely survive the disaster.*[2] [Emphasis added.]

Whom does this last sentence most remind us of, if not the Churchill of 1940—the Churchill of "never surrender"? Lady Violet Bonham Carter noted this same passage, asking: "Can there be any doubt that if in 1940 the Battle of Britain had ended in defeat we would have been one of these?"[3] How did he have the premonition, forty years before the fact, that the fate of his country might come down to the courage of such a man?

———◆◆◆———

Looking back today, Churchill seems like a figure of destiny, and yet his best-known predictions of the awful consequences of appeasement and his rise to the premiership in Britain's darkest hour are but the culmination of a lifetime of extraordinary predictions. Churchill often deprecated his own facility of foresight, once remarking, "I always avoid prophesying beforehand, because it is much better policy to prophesy after the event has already taken place." On another occasion he said the chief qualification of a politician "is the ability to foretell what is going to happen tomorrow, next week, next month, and next year. And to have the ability afterwards to explain why it didn't happen." But Churchill seldom had to explain why his warnings or predictions did not come to pass. Quite the opposite; some of his long-range predictions, especially concerning technology, are coming true right now. How did Churchill acquire this foresight? What advice did he give to anyone wishing to understand the statesman's art?

His simple and frequently repeated advice can be boiled down to two words that he shared with me when I met him while an exchange student in England in 1953: "Study history, study history." He added, "In history lie all the secrets of statecraft." It was a familiar lesson for those close to Churchill. He gave the same advice to his grandson, Winston S. Churchill II, when the boy was only eight years old. "Learn all you can about the past," Churchill wrote to his grandson in 1948, when the younger Winston was away at boarding school, "for how else can anyone make a guess about what is going to happen in the future."

I shared Churchill's advice with Richard Nixon, for whom I worked as a speechwriter. Nixon expressed his appreciation of

Churchill's skill as a prophet: "Churchill had the mind of an historian and the courage of a soldier. First, Churchill could see the patterns of the past being repeated in the present, and second, he had no fear of risking political death by going against the polls or conventional wisdom." Nixon added that "the vision of Churchill was all-encompassing as it spanned not only the world of diplomacy and politics but the sphere of technology."

A careful review of Churchill's own historical works, starting with his magisterial biography of his forebear John Churchill, the first duke of Marlborough, and continuing with his multi-volume works on the two world wars and his *History of the English-Speaking Peoples*, will show that it was not merely the repetition of past patterns of history that he could see. History for Churchill was a source of imagination about how the future would *change*, which is why he wrote, "The longer you look back, the farther you can look forward."[4] Churchill exemplifies a saying attributed to Thucydides that "history is philosophy teaching by example." The modern philosopher Isaiah Berlin wrote that Churchill had "a historical imagination so strong, so comprehensive, as to encase the whole of the present and the whole of the future in a framework of a rich and multicolored past."[5]

Churchill's historical analysis of the megalomaniacal "Sun King," Louis XIV, and his observations of Napoleon's military and political strategy clearly informed his early perception that Hitler's Nazi movement would become a worldwide threat if left unchecked. Churchill knew, as soon as the early 1920s, that the Versailles peace conference of 1919 had left Germany embittered and that Germany would strain at the leash to re-arm in defiance of the terms of Versailles. Churchill watched the feebleness of the successive Weimar governments, with instability yielding to crisis as the Great Depression spread across Europe. He had taken wary note of Hitler even before the Nazi party took power in 1933, and Churchill warned early of "the tumultuous insurgence of ferocity and war spirit" in Germany. His early warnings were not popular in a nation still deeply war weary after the colossal loss of life in World War I. His recommendations against disarmament were met with hoots and jeers from his fellow members of Parliament.

It would not be the last time that Churchill's perception of the tendency of world affairs was poorly received yet ultimately vindicated by subsequent events. The arc of his predictions about Nazi Germany and his arguments against appeasement of dictators found its sequel after World War II with his overview of the Cold War.

Not long after Churchill was turfed out of 10 Downing Street at the end of World War II, he came to the United States at the invitation of President Harry Truman to speak at Westminster College in Fulton, Missouri, the president's home state. The world was weary of war and eager to enjoy a new era of peace. Given the public mood, Churchill's warning of the new totalitarian threat in his famous "Iron Curtain" speech did not fall on sympathetic ears. Even though the president had previewed the speech during the long train ride with Churchill to Missouri and had privately expressed his approval of the message, Truman felt compelled publicly to disassociate himself from Churchill's remarks. Eleanor Roosevelt, who had never cared for Churchill during the war, called him "a warmonger," and seven Democratic senators called him a threat to world peace. Even the conservative *Wall Street Journal* criticized the Fulton address. Yet today the "Iron Curtain" speech is celebrated for its wisdom and foresight about how the West should conduct the Cold War so as to avoid World War III—advice that was, this time, largely followed. As we shall see, Churchill predicted with uncanny accuracy the duration of the Cold War and how it would end if sensible policy were followed.

Churchill's emphasis on history has led some to suppose that he was merely "a man of the past." Churchill's abiding interest in history, and the powerful imagination it produced was not simply a variation of the idea that "history repeats itself," or what social scientists call "pattern recognition." He intuited technological and social changes that no historical precedent would have suggested. He anticipated far ahead of time such features of the modern world as nuclear weapons, wireless communications, terrorism, increasingly superficial media coverage of government, and giant government bureaucracies. He could be slow to perceive or come around on some issues, such as women's suffrage. During the years when he made his living by accepting virtually every writing project offered, he declined to write a speculative article on the subject "Will there ever be a woman prime minister?"

Despite mistakes or misperceptions, Churchill's historical imagination was keenly attuned to the irregular rhythms of extraordinary change. Consider the sweep of his public life: in early adulthood he participated in the last large cavalry charge of the British army, while his career ended with his deliberations over what to do about the problem of nuclear weapons. Has any statesman's career spanned such spectacular and ominous change? *Time* magazine, in naming Churchill "Man of the Half-Century" in 1950, did not think so. "No man's history can sum up the dreadful, wonderful years, 1900–1950," *Time* wrote; "Churchill's story comes closest."

One of his political adversaries, the Labour prime minister Clement Attlee, offered a perceptive analogy to explain Churchill's genius, comparing him to a layer cake: "One layer was certainly seventeenth century. The eighteenth century in him is obvious. There was the nineteenth century, and a large slice, of course, of the twentieth century; and another, curious, layer which may possibly have been the twenty-first."[6] Churchill himself reflected in his autobiography, *My Early Life*, "I wonder often whether any other generation has seen such astounding revolutions of data and values as those through which we have lived. Scarcely anything material or established which I was brought up to believe was permanent and vital, has lasted. Everything I was sure or taught to be sure was impossible, has happened."[7]

Churchill wrote these words in 1930. Many of the most sweeping changes he had already anticipated were yet to occur. While he regarded many of the changes and events he predicted with melancholy or regret, he was never fearful. Reviewing his many prophecies is not just an exercise in recollection. As Attlee's analogy ought to suggest, studying Churchill's cast of mind should instill the same kind of hopefulness in the twenty-first century.

PART I

WORLD WAR I

CHAPTER I

PRESCIENT AS A SCHOOLBOY

CHURCHILL ENVISIONS A 1914 TRANSCONTINENTAL WAR

*"The new century will witness the great war
for the existence of the Individual."*

—CHURCHILL TO BOURKE COCKRAN,
NOVEMBER 30, 1899

When contemplating the whole of Churchill's great career,
it is important to look past the most spectacular chapter—
his "finest hour" leading Britain in World War II—and
recognize that the central issue of Churchill's entire career was the
problem of *scale* in war and peace. As his letter to Bourke Cockran—
written on his twenty-fifth birthday, a few weeks before he escaped
from a Boer POW camp—attests, Churchill saw how changes in

technology, wealth, and politics not only would create the conditions for "total war" but also would transform war into an ideological contest over the status of the individual.

Churchill was writing to Cockran, a Democratic congressman from New York City, about the economic problem of the "trusts," which was then front and center in American politics. As we shall see, Churchill had strong views about how governments would need to respond to social changes in the twentieth century—indeed, that question was the focus of his early ministerial career—but from his earliest days, even before he entered politics, he saw that the new scale of things in the modern world would be felt most powerfully in the area of warfare. His observations about the "terrible machinery of scientific war" in *The River War* led him to ask what would happen when two modern nations—not Britain and the Sudanese Dervishes—confronted each other with the modern weapons of war. It was a question no one else was asking.

Nearly every politician and military commander associated with the 1898 Sudan campaign regarded it as just another in a series of minor military skirmishes or border clashes necessary to maintaining the British Empire in the late nineteenth century. The era of epic continental warfare—of megalomaniacal ambition like that of Napoleon or Louis XIV—was thought to be over. "It seemed inconceivable," Churchill wrote later in *The World Crisis*, "that the same series of tremendous events, through which since the days of Queen Elizabeth we had three times made our way successfully, should be repeated a fourth time and on an immeasurably larger scale."[1]

This was no mere flourish of retrospection. In fact, Churchill himself had first conceived the possibility of intense conflict among the continental powers—occurring in 1914 no less—when he was a schoolboy. It was the first of several astonishing predictions of World War I.

One of the persistent misconceptions of Churchill is that he was a poor student. It is more accurate to say he was, by his own admission, a rebellious student, often bored with the curriculum and chafing under the standard teaching methods of the time. It was obvious from his earliest days in school that he was extremely bright and facile with the English language, a prodigy at learning history and extending its lessons. Still, he was often "on report," or ranked near the bottom of his class at the end of the term.

One of Churchill's instructors at Harrow, Robert Somervell, recognized the boy's abilities. In fact, Somervell thought Churchill ought to attend one of Britain's prestigious universities rather than the military academy at Sandhurst, where he eventually enrolled. When Churchill was fourteen, Somervell challenged him to write an essay on a topic of his own choosing. He wanted to give his pupil free range to see what his imagination and comprehensive knowledge of history might produce. Churchill's father, Lord Randolph, had been chancellor of the exchequer, and some speculate that Somervell, expecting an equally illustrious political career for the son, wanted to have a record for the school of Churchill's early prowess.

Churchill framed his essay as a report of a junior officer from a battlefield on which the British army was fighting Czarist Russia. The date he chose: 1914.

The Engagement of
"La Marais"
July 7th, 1914.
By an Aide de Camp of Gen. C.
Officer Commanding
H.M. Troops in R.

In his essay, which filled seventeen lined pages, Churchill manifested his knack for map-making and his knowledge of geography. He appended five pages of maps on a scale of two inches to a mile depicting the placement and movement of batteries, trenches, artillery, convoys, tents, and regiments of cavalry and infantry, as well as topography.

Churchill's essay is a personal, first-hand account of two days of combat, interspersed with personal asides. The aide-de-camp is exhausted after two days: "I am so tired that I can't write anymore now. I must add that the cavalry reconnaissance party found that there is no enemy to be seen. Now I wish for a good night, as I don't know when I get another sleep. Man may work. But man must sleep."

He describes a meeting of the junior officer with senior officers: "Aide-de-camp," said General C., "order these men to extend and advance on the double." On another occasion, the general is smashed in the head with a fragment of an artillery shell. Churchill wrote, "General C. observing his fate with a look of indifference turns to me and says 'Go yourself—aide-de-camp.'"

At times, Churchill's descriptions of battlefield carnage are suggestive of the American novelist Stephen Crane, who published his classic *The Red Badge of Courage* a few years later. The astonishing number of men killed in a single encounter foreshadowed the numbers in World War I, a quarter of a century later.

> The fields which this morning were green are now tinged with the blood of 17,000 men.... Through the veil of smoke—through the stream of wounded—over the corpses, I ride back to our lines in safety.
>
> And a crackle of musketry mixes with the cannonade. Smoke clouds drift and gather on the plain or hang over the marsh.... Bang! A puff of smoke has darted from one of their batteries and the report floats down to us on the wind; the battle has begun.

The aide-de-camp reports of his near escape from injury or death when he was dismounted in a clash with Cossack cavalry.

> I jumped on a stray horse and rode for my life. Thud! Thud! Thud! And the hoofs of a Cossack's come nearer and nearer behind me. I glance back—the point of a Cossack's lance—ahead smoke. The Cossack gains on me. A heavy blow on my back—a crash behind. The thrust strikes my pouch—does not penetrate me. The Cossack has fallen over a corpse.

As might be expected, the English army eventually routs its Russian adversaries. Despite the Czarists' initial success in a skirmish, the British infantry pushes back their counterparts on the second day of battle.

> The enemy retreated slowly and deliberately at first but at the river Volga, they became broken and our cavalry, light and heavy, executed a most brilliant charge which completed the confusion. And thus, the 63,000 Russians fled across the Volga in disorder pursued by 6,000 cavalry and 40,000 infantry.

Churchill concludes with an observation of "the superiority of the English lion over the Russian bear."

Churchill's Harrow essay is exhibited today in the underground War Rooms in London, where Churchill managed World War II during the Blitz.

CHAPTER 2

WARNINGS FROM
A YOUNG MP

DEMOCRATIC WARFARE WILL BE
ALL-ENCOMPASSING

Churchill's youthful essay predicting an epic military clash on the continent was only the first instance of his foreseeing the First World War. The second occurred at the beginning of his long political career.

Taking his place in 1901 as the youngest member of Parliament and a member of his father's Conservative Party, Churchill immediately made his mark with several notable—some critics said impertinent—speeches about the Boer War and other colonial affairs.

As did his service in the Sudan, his service in the Boer War awakened his imagination to the possibilities of modern warfare, and he was not sanguine about them. His experience in the battle of Spion

Kop in January 1900 was notably different from that in the battle of
Omdurman in the Sudan less than two years before because of one
simple factor: the Boers, unlike the Dervishes, had modern armaments, which exacted a terrible toll on the attacking British forces,
despite Britain's superior numbers. In fact, Churchill thought the Boers
had superior battlefield rifles, and as for artillery Churchill observed
that "one Boer gun usually managed to do to our men as much harm
as six British guns do harm to the Boers."[1] It was the first glimmer of
a central principle that Churchill stressed in World War I—the superiority of defensive positions. It was a principle he could not get the
British generals to absorb sufficiently.

After Britain's initial success storming the heights of Spion Kop,
the ferocious Boer counterattack forced a costly retreat. The dead
piled up three deep on the slope. Lieutenant Winston Churchill was
in the middle of the fight, trying to rally the troops. "The scenes on
Spion Kop were among the strangest and most terrible I have ever
witnessed," Churchill wrote to a friend. "Corpses lay here and there.
Many of the wounds were of a horrible nature. The splinters and
fragments of the shell had torn and mutilated in the most ghastly
manner."[2] It was yet another small-scale preview of the dreadful
character of the Great War that would come in the following decade—
right down to the all-important detail of the lack of battlefield
leadership by the junior officer corps on the spot.

Churchill's experience in these previews of the mass slaughter of
modern warfare was complemented by what he had learned of the
American Civil War from his mother's side of the family. While the
British had not yet suffered the trauma of the young manhood of
whole towns being decimated by war, Churchill had seen first hand,
in his North American visits, the hundreds of stone markers bearing
the names of the Civil War dead in upstate New York towns, some
with populations of only a thousand.

From his own experience in the British army in India, the Sudan, and South Africa, Churchill gained two insights that would become important in his long political career: a recognition of the increasing horrors of modern warfare and a disdain for what he saw as the shortsightedness of much of the military establishment. It is often said of Churchill in World War II that "he interfered with the generals." Quite true! In his third major speech to the House of Commons in 1901, Churchill said "I had always been led to believe that the generals existed for the Army, and not the Army for the generals." He had acquired some of his instincts from his father, Lord Randolph Churchill, who had warned with extraordinary prescience in 1886, "A wise foreign policy will extricate England from Continental struggles and keep her outside of German, Russian, French, or Austrian disputes."

It should not have been a surprise that the young MP would openly oppose his own party's proposal for an expansion of the army. In the spring of 1901, the secretary of state for war, St. John Brodrick, proposed a scheme of army "reform" that amounted to a significant increase in expenditures in order to equip six additional army corps. If adopted, the additional expense would represent a near doubling of the army's budget over the previous eight years.

Churchill thought the proposal was unsound on multiple grounds. First, the Conservative Party, if it were worthy of its name, ought to stand for frugality. The proposal seemed to open the way to profligate spending by every department of the government. On May 13, 1901, Churchill took to the floor of the House to deliver a stinging attack on what he called "the costly, trumpery, dangerous military playthings on which the Secretary of State for War has set his heart."

Churchill asked: "Has the wealth of the country doubled? Has the population of the Empire doubled? Have the armies of Europe doubled? Is there no poverty at home? Has the English Channel dried up and we are no longer an island?" At this point in his political career, Churchill was more concerned with social reform and the establishment of social insurance programs, as we shall see. Separately Churchill had complained, "I see little glory in an Empire which can rule the waves and is unable to flush its sewers." This puts in relief his argument against increasing spending on a secondary component of national security.

> I hold it is unwise to have no regard to the fact that in this reform we are diverting national resources from their proper channel of development. It may be argued that if other nations increase their armed forces so must we. If you look into the tangled mass of figures on the subject you will find that while other nations during the last fifteen years have been increasing their navies we have been increasing our expenditure on our Army, which is not after all our most important weapon.... My contention is that we are spending too much money on armaments, and so may impair our industries; but that if the money has to be spent, then it would be better to spend it on the Fleet than on the Army.

This last comment was based on Churchill's view that England and its Empire depended first and foremost on the navy for its defense. This was another minor prophesy of Churchill's that would soon find vindication. In just a few years, Churchill was running the Royal Navy as First Lord of the Admiralty, and his most pressing challenge was Germany's sudden and aggressive buildup of its navy.

"This is not an Army reform," Churchill continued, "but an Army increase." The needs of defending "the minor emergencies" that occur on "the varied frontiers of the Empire" could easily be accomplished with one more army corps, but the expansion Brodrick wanted would be wholly inadequate for a general European war. "But we must not expect to meet the great civilized Powers in this easy fashion. We must not regard war with a modern Power as a kind of game in which we may take a hand, and with good luck and good management may play adroitly for an evening and come safe home with our winnings. It is not that, and I rejoice that it cannot be that. *A European war cannot be anything but a cruel, heartrending struggle*...." Brodrick's additional army corps, Churchill added, would not protect Britain in the event of a European war, because they were too small: "If we are in danger, they will not make us safe. They are enough to irritate; they are not enough to overawe."

It was not merely that European war would be larger in scale than the frontier wars of the Empire that Churchill had witnessed in India and Africa. England had successfully prosecuted such European conflicts against Napoleon just a century before. The wars of the twentieth century would be different for two reasons—science and democracy. These would make for a century of Total War. As Churchill noted, "if we are ever to enjoy the bitter fruits of victory, [a European war] must demand, perhaps for several years, the whole manhood of the nation, the entire suspension of peaceful industries, and the concentrating to one end of every vital energy in the community." Churchill professed himself "astonished... to hear with what composure and how glibly Members, and even Ministers, talk of a European war."

Gone were "the former days" when the causes of war were the ambitions, passions, or petty political intrigues of kings or ministers, whose wars "were fought by small regular armies of professional soldiers," whose style and smaller scale of warfare made it "possible to limit the liabilities of the combatants." Continuing with his theme of science and scale, Churchill came to his climax:

> But now, when mighty populations are impelled against each other, each individual severally embittered and enflamed—when the resources of science and civilization sweep away everything that might mitigate their fury, a European war can only end in the ruin of the vanquished and the scarcely less fatal commercial dislocation and exhaustion of the conquerers.

Churchill then uttered one of the most incisive prophecies of his long career: "Democracy is more vindictive than Cabinets. The wars of peoples will be more terrible than those of kings."

Churchill's speech thrilled the Liberal Party opposition (which he joined a few years later in his first party switch), and annoyed much of his own party's leadership, who thought he was merely pursuing a posthumous vindication of his father. But he succeeded in his object: Brodrick's army scheme was shelved. Brodrick resigned and was sent to the India Office. Churchill had signaled to Conservative Party leadership that the independent young man wielded an influence with which they would have to reckon. More than one observer thought he was likely to become prime minister some day. He was only twenty-six years old.

While this was a minor early triumph for Churchill, very few took to heart his warning about the character of war in the twentieth century. The conventional wisdom was that, for economic reasons, a protracted continental war was impossible. Churchill proved himself a much better prophet than Karl Marx and his followers, who thought the coming of war would hasten the revolution of the working classes in capitalist democracies and weaken nationalist sentiments. Just the opposite occurred; the coming of war saw a swelling of patriotic fervor among all classes. As Churchill later observed in *The World Crisis*, "For a year after the war had begun hardly anyone understood how terrific, and almost inexhaustible were the resources in force, in substance, in virtue, behind every one of the combatants. The vials of wrath were full: but so were the reservoirs of power.... When it was all over, Torture and Cannibalism were the only two expedients that the civilized, scientific, Christian States had been able to deny themselves: and these were of doubtful utility."[3]

Churchill's prophetic insights into the coming conflagration were not exhausted. As the dread year of 1914 approached, his predictions grew more precise.

CHAPTER 3

A FATEFUL MEMORANDUM

CHURCHILL OUTLINES GERMANY'S ATTACK PLAN—THREE YEARS BEFOREHAND

C hurchill is best known, apart from his great wartime speeches, for his pre-war attacks on appeasement and his demands that Britain re-arm to face the growing Nazi menace. Because of those positions and his post-war advocacy of the alliance against the Soviet Union, he was often accused of being a "warmonger"—an unjust calumny. One of the most thoughtful defenses of appeasement came from Churchill himself. In a speech during the Korean War, Churchill said, "Appeasement in itself may be good or bad according to the circumstances. Appeasement from weakness and fear is alike futile and fatal. Appeasement from strength might be the surest and perhaps the only path to world peace." And he adopted one of his father's slogans: "Peace, Retrenchment, and Reform."

Churchill's stance in the debate over "Mr. Brodrick's Army" illustrates two attitudes toward the military that characterized his entire career. First, Churchill did not defer to the military establishment. On the contrary, he consistently questioned military orthodoxy. One of his legendary quips is supposed to have come in response to an admiral who protested that Churchill was interfering with the traditions of the navy. He replied, "Tradition, I tell you what the tradition of the Royal Navy is: Rum, sodomy, and the lash." (Churchill's official biographer, Sir Martin Gilbert, doubts the authenticity of this remark, but it has long been an accepted part of Churchill lore.) He was also an innovator in military technology and doctrine, as we shall see.

Churchill's other characteristic attitude was his opposition, during peacetime, to building armaments for armaments' sake. He thought such expenditures diverted too much taxpayer money from more pressing domestic social needs. Over the course of Churchill's entire political career, he supported lower defense spending most of the time. He was one of the authors of the "ten-year rule," according to which British defense planning should look ten years ahead for potential conflicts, and plan accordingly. If no conflict could reasonably be foreseen, Churchill usually urged restraint in defense spending. But when the potential for serious conflict began to appear on the horizon, as it did before each world war, Churchill bowed to reality and urged preparedness.

Such a moment came in 1911, when Churchill was serving as Home Secretary in the cabinet of Prime Minister Herbert Asquith. Appointed at age thirty-five, he was the second-youngest Home Secretary in history. This post kept Churchill preoccupied with domestic affairs with the never-ending troubles in Ireland. When the navy in 1909 pressed for six new battleships in response to the German buildup, Churchill joined the cabinet opponents in trying to hold the number to four. With typical wit, Churchill described the outcome: "In the end a curious and characteristic solution was reached. The

Admiralty had demanded six ships: the economists offered four: and we finally compromised on eight." Churchill believed that Germany was badly overextending itself, having doubled its national debt over the previous ten years. Germany was rapidly approaching its limits, he thought, though he allowed for the possibility that it might pursue foreign adventurism as an answer for its economic problems. In a memorandum to the cabinet in 1909, Churchill mused, "...a period of internal strain approaches in Germany. Will the tension be relieved by moderation or snapped by calculated violence?.... [O]ne of the two courses must be taken soon." This was, Churchill wrote later in *The World Crisis*, "the first sinister impression that I was ever led to record."

But then came the Agadir crisis of 1911, which proved to be a watershed for Churchill. In July, Germany shocked Europe with the announcement that it had sent a gunboat to the Moroccan port city of Agadir, ostensibly to "protect German interests." Germany had long complained of ill treatment by Britain, France, and Spain in its African colonial claims, but Germany took everyone by surprise with its gunboat. "All the alarm bells throughout Europe began immediately to quiver," Churchill wrote. Was this the beginning of the "calculated violence" Churchill had pondered two years before? Churchill's great Liberal Party friend, David Lloyd George, known as a pacifist, gave a rousing speech that threatened war against Germany.

Lloyd George's speech had the desired sobering effect on Germany. Old-fashioned quiet diplomacy—perhaps the last of the nineteenth-century style—resolved the crisis, but the war drums had sounded, and Britain's military planners had begun contemplating how a war against Germany might be conducted. A few days before a key meeting of the Committee of Imperial Defense, Churchill set down in a long memorandum how a war on the continent would begin. "It was," Churchill wrote later, "only an attempt to pierce the veil of the future; to conjure up in the mind a vast imaginary situation; to balance the incalculable; to weigh the imponderable."

In his paper, Churchill envisioned an opening battle in which the alliance of Britain, France, and Russia would confront an attack by the Central Powers of Germany and Austria. In such a situation, Churchill concluded, the decisive military operations would be between France and Germany. "The German army," he said, "mobilizes 2,200,000 against 1,700,000 for the French." Germany would attack through neutral Belgium, over the Meuse River, into northern France. "The balance of probability," predicted Churchill, "is that by the twentieth day the French armies will have been driven from the line of the Meuse and would be falling back on Paris and the south." He reasoned that the thrust of the German advance would then be weakened because of diminishing supplies and increasing casualties as it pressed southward.

As the war progressed, losses to the French army would require the deployment of French troops from other regions to reinforce the defenses south of Paris. By the thirtieth day, the arrival of the British army, together with growing pressure from Russia, would slow the German advance.

The result, said Churchill, would be that "by the fortieth day, Germany should be extended at full strain...on her warfront," stress that would become "more severe and ultimately overwhelming," unless, improbably, the Germans had achieved a quick victory. It was then that "opportunities for the decisive trial of strength may occur."

Churchill recommended that Britain send 107,000 men to France at the outbreak of the war; 100,000 troops should depart from India on the first day in order to reach Marseilles by the fortieth day. Churchill circulated the memorandum "with the hope that if the unfavorable prediction about the twentieth day had been borne out, so also would be the favorable prediction about the fortieth day."

Upon receiving the memorandum, General Henry Wilson told the Imperial Defense Committee that Churchill's prediction was "ridiculous and fantastic—a silly memorandum." Unexpressed was the general's contempt for an idea from someone who had never risen above the rank of lieutenant.

Despite the scorn of the army staff, in three years, it would all happen just as Churchill predicted. He gave the twentieth day of the German offensive as the day on which the French armies would be driven from the Meuse and forecasted that the German army's advance would be stopped on the fortieth. This is exactly what happened, and on the forty-first day, Germany lost the Battle of the Marne, setting the stage for the awful stalemate of trench warfare for the next four years.

"This was one of the most prescient strategic documents that Churchill ever wrote," his son Randolph recorded decades later in the official biography. When Arthur Balfour, sometimes a critic of Churchill, re-read this memo shortly after the outbreak of the war in September 1914, he wrote to Churchill's private secretary, "It is a triumph of prophecy!" More importantly, the Agadir crisis had re-awakened in Churchill his previously expressed worries about the prospect of total war between modern nations. It caused him to change his mind about his earlier opposition to a naval buildup. He wrote in retrospect that "although the Chancellor of the Exchequer and I were right in the narrow sense [about the number of battleships], we were absolutely wrong in relation to the deep tides of destiny."[1] Churchill's political focus would now change from domestic to foreign affairs, where it would remain for most of the rest of his life.

This memorandum and other actions of Churchill around the time of the Agadir crisis made the prime minister, H. H. Asquith, realize that Churchill needed a more prominent government post from which to influence the nation's strategic destiny. Within a few weeks of the resolution of the Agadir crisis, Asquith had elevated Churchill to First Lord of the Admiralty, in which office Churchill introduced a number of forward-looking reforms and innovations that echo down to the present day.

CHAPTER 4

OPPOSING THE SANGUINE MAJORITY

WWI WILL BE A DRAWN-OUT CONFLICT

The scope and horror of World War I caught everyone by surprise—everyone except Churchill. Enlightened, cosmopolitan opinion thought that a long, total war was, for economic reasons, impossible. When the war came in August 1914, nearly everyone was optimistic that the war would be over quickly and cheaply—everyone except Churchill.

An account of a conversation among Churchill and other senior members of the government on the night of August 5, 1914—the day Kaiser Wilhelm refused the ultimatum to withdraw from Belgium and war was declared—reveals the naïve optimism of Britain's leaders. It was a dinner meeting at the Savoy Hotel of the Other Club, which Churchill had founded with F. E. Smith (later Lord Birkenhead), a fellow MP. The conversation turned to the new war.

The dinner party included David Lloyd George, then chancellor of the exchequer, and the secretary of state for war, Lord Kitchener, the same commander of British forces in the Sudan whom Churchill had criticized sharply in 1899 in *The River War*. Churchill and Kitchener were cordial, but there was deep enmity between them. Lloyd George, preoccupied with liberal social reforms, was gloomy about the war's implications for his domestic spending plans, but Kitchener was optimistic: "Bunch of old men and young boys—that's all the Boche have," said the general. "It'll be over in four months."

Churchill reportedly growled, "More likely four years."

In the first week of the war, the British sprang to arms with medieval valor. Officers looked forward to acquitting themselves gallantly and expected to defeat the Germans in Belgium with dispatch. Churchill watched as the generals, thinking themselves infallible, played with their armies as if they were toy soldiers. The army was taking control of the war away from the politicians. When one general opined that no one with less than forty years in the field should have a hand in running the war, Churchill observed that such a rule would have disqualified Alexander the Great, Hannibal, Julius Caesar, Cromwell, Marlborough, and Napoleon.

The greatest failure of strategy, Churchill thought, was France's rather than Britain's. He was certain that the French would try to preserve their maneuverability, striking the advancing German army opportunistically as it overextended itself. "I did not, of course, contemplate that the French would dig one uniform line along the whole length of their frontier," Churchill wrote. Unknown to the British, the secret French strategy, code named "Plan XVII," was to counterattack Germany through the northeast with all their remaining reserves, on the theory that the Germans could not or would not break through from Belgium. "Both these calculations were to be completely falsified by the first events of the war," Churchill wrote; "By the evening of the 23rd [of September], 'Plan XVII' had failed in every single element."

As the early weeks of the war unfolded exactly as Churchill had predicted and the outline of a stalemate came into view, Kitchener quickly came around to Churchill's point of view. Kitchener told a cabinet meeting that, as Churchill recalled, "Everyone expected that the war would be short; but wars took unexpected courses, and we must now prepare for a long struggle.... We must be prepared to put armies of millions in the field and maintain them for several years."

As the tragedy unfolded, Churchill addressed the National Liberal Club in mid-September, warning, "This war will be long and somber. It will have many reverses of fortune and many hopes falsified by subsequent events." The stalemate had hardened by Christmas of 1914, and Churchill increasingly despaired that the military leadership, failing to grasp the dimensions of the disaster, were tamely submitting to the awful arithmetic of "attrition." He recoiled at the thought of hundreds of thousands in wet trenches full of lice and vermin dying from poison gas, massed machine gun fire, and aerial strafing. He could see that the generals were perfectly content to throw away the young manhood of the nation on a fruitless strategy. In an impassioned letter to the prime minister, H. H. Asquith, Churchill wrote:

> I think it is quite possible that neither side will have the strength to penetrate the other's line in the Western theatre.... My impression is that the position of both armies is not likely to undergo any decisive change—although no doubt several hundred thousand men will be spent to satisfy the military mind on the point.... On the assumption that these views are correct, the question arises, how ought we to apply our growing military power? Are there not other alternatives than sending our armies to chew barbed wire in Flanders?

Churchill thought there were two answers to this problem—one strategic and one technological. The strategic principle stayed with him for the rest of his life and shaped many of his perceptions and actions in World War II. "Battles are won by slaughter and maneuver," Churchill wrote. "The greater the general, the more he contributes in maneuver, the less he demands in slaughter." Since there were no flanks to be turned on the western front, Churchill posed the question to Asquith: "If it is impossible or unduly costly to pierce the German lines on existing fronts, ought we not, as new forces come to hand, to engage him on new frontiers?" The answer Churchill offered was a naval expedition through the Dardanelles, with the objective of knocking Turkey out of the war and opening a new front for Russian forces in the east.

When the Ottoman Empire entered the war on the side of Germany on October 31, 1914, Churchill immediately raised the idea of an attack on Constantinople as a means of freeing the Czarist army to concentrate on pressing Germany on its eastern front. If such a plan had been carried out immediately, Germany might have been defeated in 1915. It is only necessary to consult a map to understand the importance of Constantinople, which was the London or Berlin of the Near East. The capture of this gateway to the Balkans would have a profound influence on Bulgaria, Romania, and Greece—or on Italy, still neutral at that time but leaning in the direction of the Allies.

Churchill's conception of such an invasion was a joint military and naval operation. Kitchener was not sold on the idea, but by January, when Russia was urgently appealing for British help against the Turks, he changed his mind. Kitchener urged Churchill to undertake this naval bombardment, but he was not ready to take British troops out of France to launch a concerted action.

On the pledge that troops would be forthcoming, Churchill sent a flotilla to the Straits of the Dardanelles leading to Constantinople. The admiral leading the assault called off his marine invading force after they collided with a few mines. Churchill pleaded for the assault to continue, but the admirals in London overruled him. If they had continued, later investigation proved, they would have met little resistance, since the Turkish gun crews had run out of ammunition. The result was a lull in the campaign until Kitchener could mobilize some troops for an assault. In April, Kitchener had in his command new volunteer troops from Australia and New Zealand. They were called "Anzacs."

The Anzac landing on the Gallipoli peninsula on May 15 met with disaster. During the six-week pause, the Germans had reinforced the Turkish defenses with machine gun batteries on the embankments with barbed wire below. Twenty-five thousand Australians and New Zealanders were simply mowed down. It was a classic case of too little too late, and the scapegoat was the First Lord of the Admiralty. For the opposition Conservative Party, it was payback time for a defector from their ranks. Asquith and Kitchener were spared the vitriolic attacks Churchill received. One graphic example of the vilification of Churchill was a political cartoon showing an impish little boy gleefully throwing faggots (Australians and New Zealanders) into a bonfire.

Churchill resigned his ministry and joined the army as a major in France. The failure of the Dardanelles offensive was a black mark on Churchill's reputation for decades. But even some of his political opponents recognized that the blame was unfair. The leader of the Labour Party, Clement Attlee, later told Churchill that the Dardanelles initiative was "the only imaginative strategic idea of the war. I only wish that you had had full power to carry it to success."

Like his strategic understanding, Churchill's technological foresight was slow to be recognized and was misapplied for some of the same reasons the Dardanelles initiative failed: military leaders did not understand Churchill's insights, as we shall see presently.

PART II

MODERN MILITARY WEAPONS

CHAPTER 5

PREDICTING THE AGE OF AIR POWER

CHURCHILL PERCEIVES THE MILITARY POTENTIAL OF AVIATION

The history of technological innovation is filled with examples of new technologies whose full implications or best uses were only slowly recognized. Thomas Watson of IBM famously said there would be little market for home desktop computers. Even as recently as 2010, many technology seers thought there would be limited public appetite for tablet computers like the iPad.

Churchill was always far ahead of his contemporaries in anticipating how new technologies would be used, and what effect they would have on social life and warfare. For example, when advancements in submarine design in the first decade of the twentieth century spurred more construction (especially by Germany), most naval experts thought submarines would be used exclusively for coastal and harbor defense of the homeland and to break the close blockades that were the specialty of the Royal Navy. Churchill was nearly alone in recognizing that torpedo-equipped German submarines would become a potent *offensive* weapon, ranging far into the open sea, interdicting vital shipping, and posing a threat to the British surface fleet. Churchill warned of this possibility as early as 1912, but the naval establishment dismissed his unorthodox prediction.

The story of air power—with whose development Churchill was closely involved—is similar. Indeed he deserves to be considered the first political prophet of air power. Not only was he the first parliamentarian or cabinet minister to fly a plane, he became the first head of government to own a pilot's license.

The motorcar never replaced horses in the affections of the polo-playing former cavalry officer. Yet curiously, as a young man, Churchill became fascinated with the possibilities of flight that opened up in 1903 with the Wright brothers' feat at Kitty Hawk, North Carolina.

On February 25, 1909, Churchill, as president of the Board of Trade, told the cabinet, "aviation would be most important in the future" and recommended "we should place ourselves in communication with Mr. [Orville] Wright and avail ourselves of his knowledge."

A year later, when the *Daily Mail* asked for funds to back the first transatlantic flight, Churchill provided a check for ten thousand pounds. This made possible the flight of two English aviators from Newfoundland to Ireland in 1910, many years before Lindbergh's more celebrated solo flight.

By contrast, that same year General Foch of France voiced the opinion that prevailed throughout the military when he derided the use of airplanes in battle: "It's just a sport—the aeroplane—it is a zero in war."

As First Lord of the Admiralty, on November 10, 1913, Churchill chose air power as his subject for a speech at the prestigious Lord Mayor's Banquet at the Guildhall in London:

I have come here tonight to tell you that it is not only in naval aeroplanes that we must have superiority. I would venture to submit to this great company assembled that the enduring safety of this country will not be maintained by force of arms unless over the whole sphere of aerial development we are able to make ourselves the first nation.... [C]ommand and perfection will be indispensable elements not only in naval strength but in national security.

A half year later, as tensions between Britain and Imperial Germany heightened, Churchill was already taking steps to make a flying service an integral part of the Royal Navy, while the War Office was drawing up contingency plans for dispatching men on horseback to France.

At a dinner at the Savoy Hotel, Churchill told his audience: "This new art and science of flying is surely one in which Great Britain ought to be able to show itself, I do not say supreme in numbers, but supreme in quality.... One cannot doubt that the development of the flying art...must in the future exercise a potent influence...on the military destinies of states."

Churchill practiced what he preached. Two years before, in the Admiralty, he had founded the Royal Navy Air Service—a forerunner of the Royal Flying Corps, and later the Royal Air Force. (The United States Air Force, by contrast, originated in World War II with the Army Air Corps.)

Because of Churchill's endeavors, Britain became the first nation to arm a plane with a machine gun and the first to launch an airborne torpedo. Churchill even ordered a test version of a helicopter. It was Churchill who gave to the English language the word "seaplane" and coined the word "flight" to designate the deployment of four aircraft in the skies. Another phrase born of his fertile pen was "the fog of war," through which only planes could pierce from their sky view above.

His responsibility in command, as well as his curiosity, impelled him to become a pilot himself. His first trip in a seaplane was in 1912. At that time the danger of death accompanied any flight, but of course, the risk only added to the thrill of adventure for Churchill. The next week he demanded his first lesson as a pilot. The following day his instructor was killed while piloting the same machine.

A month later, Churchill piloted a new type of seaplane off Southampton and landed safely. Yet the same plane crashed a week later. Members of Parliament then communicated to the prime minister the folly of a cabinet minister jeopardizing his life by his flying ventures. "I regret," answered Asquith, "that valuable lives should be exposed to needless risks, but I have no reason to suppose that I have any such persuasive influence on the Right Honourable Member."

Neither did his terrified wife. Churchill wrote from Eastchurch Naval Flying Center after going up three times. "Darling—We have had a very jolly day in the air." She wired her alarm ending, "I hope my telegram hasn't vexed you, but please be kind and don't fly any more just now."

Her plea was disregarded. In 1913, he was going up about ten times a day. The naval pilots were as fearful as his wife. Thirty-two was regarded as the top age of a pilot, and Churchill was then thirty-eight.

After Clementine's frantic urging, Churchill's closest friend, F. E. Smith, wrote, "Why do you do such a foolish thing as fly repeatedly? Surely it's unfair to your family, your career, and your friends."

One airman Churchill ordered to go up with him as co-pilot arrived a bit late for their afternoon flight. "Where have you been?" growled Churchill. "Making a will," replied the man cheerfully.

If Churchill had robust faith in the future offensive use of the airplane, he had little faith in the dirigible. The Germans were building a fleet of Zeppelins, but Churchill resisted pleas to mount a counterforce in Britain. "I rate the Zeppelin much lower as a weapon of war than anyone else," he responded. "I believe that this enormous bladder of combustible and explosive gas would prove easily destructible."

When World War I broke out, Churchill ordered his seaplanes to bomb the Zeppelin air sheds at Cologne and Friedrichshaven. The dirigibles were useful for observing British defenses and deployment of troops, and he made sure that a lot of them would never take to the skies. At the same time, his seaplanes bombed to smithereens the U-boat bases at Zeebrugge. The War Office, which had doubted the efficacy of air power, commended the bombing as "sound and justified."

Churchill, in 1917, was appointed by the new prime minister, David Lloyd George, to the new position of secretary of state for munitions and supplies, as well as secretary of state for the new Ministry of Air—the first such department in the world. Shortly afterward, in a speech in Bedford, a center of the manufacturing engine industry, Churchill identified his chief goal—producing "masses of guns, mountains of shells, and clouds of planes."

He immediately made contact with Bernard Baruch, the chairman of U.S. War Industries, and inked a hundred-million-pound contract for American arms. Churchill's new department numbered twelve thousand civil servants and fifty groups or sub-departments, which he quickly reduced to ten.

Churchill's position at the head of the new air force department enabled him to do what no other war minister has ever done, before or since. Almost every weekday, Churchill would fly in his biplane from London to look over the battlefields in France in order to pinpoint exactly where weaponry and supplies were needed. He would return to Parliament the same evening to report his findings to the House of Commons. Today, almost a decade short of the hundredth anniversary of World War I, only a few executives pilot themselves daily to their office. Yet Churchill was commuting daily from his

ministry in London to the western front in France and back to the
House of Commons that night.

It should be mentioned that, in 1918, he ceased his daily flying
after his third plane crash. The word from his wife reportedly was
"either the aeroplane or Clementine." Churchill later mused, "The
air is an extremely dangerous mistress. Once under its spell, most
lovers are faithful to the end, which is not always old age."

Before taking office in the spring of 1917, with the war in a stalemate, Churchill proclaimed in a speech in Dundee, "Complete unques-
tionable supremacy in the air would give an overwhelming advantage."
It was a prediction that found its vindication in World War II.

CHAPTER 6

CHURCHILL DEVELOPS THE TANK

SURMOUNTING TRENCH WARFARE

N ew technologies have changed the character of warfare since the rock gave way to the first spear. Some innovations, like castles and moats, tipped the advantage to the defense. The longbow, mounted cavalry, and cannons tipped the advantage to the offense. World War I was no exception. "The present war," Churchill wrote, "has revolutionized all military theories about the field of fire. The power of the rifle is so great that 100 yards is sufficient to stop any rush and, in order to avoid the severity of artillery fire, trenches are dug.... The consequence is that war has become short range instead of long range...and opposing trenches get even closer together for mutual safety from each other's artillery fire."

Churchill's perception that advances in weaponry favored the defensive side led to a strikingly simple alternative to "chewing barbed wire in Flanders." "The mechanical danger," he wrote to Asquith, "must be overcome by a mechanical remedy.... As we could not go around the trenches, it was evidently necessary to go over them."

Since military action was not going to be a long march across plains, as in the battles of previous centuries, there had to be, explained Churchill, a way of "getting across 100 or 200 yards of open space and wire entanglements." Within six weeks of the outbreak of the war, Churchill thought he could see the answer.

Churchill's solution was a "tractor with small armored shelters in which men and machine guns could be placed which would be bullet-proof...." The singular advantage, Churchill insisted, would be "the caterpillar system [that] would enable trenches to be crossed quite easily and the weight of the machine would destroy all wire entanglements."

Churchill was perhaps a Renaissance man, but he was not a mechanical engineer; the War Board treated his creation with derision. The First Lord of the Admiralty, however, continued his experiments with his caterpillar-tracked armored vehicle. On his own initiative Churchill dedicated Admiralty funds to form a "Landship Committee" to pursue what was going to be a weapon for the army. "The matter was entirely outside the scope of my own Department or of any normal powers which I possessed," Churchill acknowledged.

Churchill's new weapon reflected his characteristic combination of ancient and modern imagination. "Think of the elephants of Roman times," he wrote. "These are mechanical elephants to break wire and earthwork phalanges." Prototypes were tested in secret inside a large naval supply warehouse marked with a sign that read "tank," indicating that it was used for making water carriers. Thus "tank" came to replace the First Lord of the Admiralty's original designation of "landship."

Functionaries in the Admiralty could not see what a vehicle for trench warfare had to do with either the Royal Navy or the new Air Service, but they did not cross swords with the First Lord, who, after all, would take all the blame if the "tank" proved to be "Winston's Folly," as critics claimed.

On February 20, 1915, the Landship Committee met in the flu-stricken Churchill's bedroom in Admiralty House. The tests had developed an armored vehicle with superior steel plating, an improved internal combustion engine, and caterpillar tracks. With the committee's recommendation, Churchill persuaded Asquith to appropriate seventy thousand pounds for the manufacture of eighteen tanks. But when the first such contraption rattled its way across the Horse Guard's Parade Route for inspection in 1915, the War Office was not impressed. Surely the mud of the trenches would swallow up "Winston's Folly."

The generals could not see the butterfly beauty concealed in the ugly caterpillar. They could not imagine that the tank could surmount the trenches in which Britain and France had suffered over a million casualties by the end of 1914. One French officer said, "Wouldn't it be easier to flood the Artois [River] and get your fleet in there?" The perimeters of geography and the sheer mass of men mobilized had constricted the generals' scope of ideas. Any innovation or inventiveness that might end the senseless killing was precluded from consideration in 1915.

By May 1915, the counsel of Britain's most farsighted and brilliant strategist was no longer heard in the War Cabinet. The Dardanelles disaster had seen to Churchill's exile, and the promising tank program atrophied in his absence. The man Churchill put in charge of the tank program wrote to him in dismay, "After losing the great advantage of your influence, I had considerable difficulty in steering the scheme past the rocks of opposition and the more insidious shoals of apathy."

Churchill had urged that the tank not be used in battle until it was ready in large numbers: "Apply them when all is ready on the largest possible scale, and with the priceless advantage of surprise." Churchill's suggestion was ignored. Tanks were first used on the Somme in 1917, but only fifteen of them. While they were effective on the battlefield, there were not enough of them to take the field and achieve a breakthrough. "My poor 'land battleships' have been let off prematurely and on a petty scale," Churchill lamented.

Churchill returned to the cabinet in 1917 as secretary of state for munitions and supplies, as well as minister for the new Air Force Department. Churchill was able to revive the tank program and saw that close to five tanks were put into the fray. In August 1918, the Hindenburg line was broken by 456 tanks rolling over the German defenses and scattering the German troops. Marshal Ludendorff would describe it as the black day of the German army. It was the turning point of the war. So often a new type of warfare introduced in the closing stage of a war will dominate the opening stage of the next war. The Nazi Blitzkrieg of tank battalions in 1939 would prove that military maxim.

It was Lloyd George who brought Churchill back into the cabinet after his exile following the Dardanelles disaster, and Lloyd George paid tribute to Churchill's initiative in creating the tank: "[T]hese suggestions [for the tank] would never have fructified had it not been for the fact that Mr. Churchill, who was then First Lord of the Admiralty, gave practical effect to them by making the necessary experiments, setting up committees for carrying the suggestions into effect, and by putting the whole of his energy and strength towards materializing the hopes of those who had been looking forward to an attempt of this kind." A special Royal Commission on War Inventions later praised Churchill, observing that "it was primarily due to the receptivity, courage, and driving force" that the idea of the tank "was converted into a practical shape."

CHAPTER 7

FORESEEING THE INVENTION OF NUCLEAR WEAPONS

HE DIVINES THE TECHNOLOGY AND ITS RAMIFICATIONS

n the aftermath of World War I, few people could imagine greater horror or carnage than Europe had just experienced. If this was not Armageddon, it was as close as the world was ever going to come. The optimists hoped it would turn out to have been "the war to end all wars," while the less optimistic hoped that the strong current of pacifism the war generated would hold war fever in check.

Churchill did not take up this facile optimism. Though he supported the League of Nations and was always hopeful about diplomatic efforts, he foresaw the possibility of "a world of monstrous shadows moving in convulsive combinations through vistas of fathomless catastrophe." Among Churchill's remarkable predictions was the possibility of nuclear weapons, perhaps delivered by missile. He made this prediction in 1924, well before the first experiments in nuclear fission were conducted. Churchill had no background—and certainly no degree—in physics or engineering.

In the 1920s, Churchill wrote a series of melancholy essays and magazine feature articles, many of them subsequently collected and published as *Amid These Storms* in Great Britain and as *Thoughts and Adventures* in the United States. Three of the essays in particular command our attention: "Shall We All Commit Suicide?", "Mass Effects in Modern Life," and "Fifty Years Hence." We shall come back to these three essays again and again in the coming chapters.

"Shall We All Commit Suicide?" was an extended version of the closing chapter of Churchill's multi-volume survey of World War I, *The World Crisis*, in which he warned, "It was not until the dawn of the twentieth century of the Christian era that War really began to enter into its kingdom as the potential destroyer of the human race." Before speculating about the efficient, material, or technological causes of this specter, Churchill reflected on the moral lessons of this change: "Mankind has never been in this position before. Without having improved appreciably in virtue or enjoying wiser guidance, it has got into its hand for the first time the tools by which it can unfailingly accomplish its own extermination."

What might be the means of this extermination? Churchill discussed what was already familiar: poison gas and chemical warfare in general. "As for poison gas… only the first chapter has been written of a terrible book." Churchill went on to speculate about how biological agents such as anthrax might be developed and weaponized—a prospect very much on the minds of the world's security services in the wake of 9/11.

These speculations required no special insight or knowledge. His others, however, are truly extraordinary. He mentions the possibility that a war might be fought with electricity, which sounds tolerably close to the contemporary worry about the effects of an electromagnetic pulse attack on a nation's electric grid. Then comes this passage:

Then there are Explosives. Have we reached the end? Has
Science turned its last page on them? May there not be
methods of using explosive energy incomparably more
intense than anything heretofore discovered? Might not a
bomb no bigger than an orange be found to possess a secret
power to destroy a whole block of buildings—nay, to concentrate the force of a thousand tons of cordite and blast
a township at a stroke? Could not explosives even of the
conventional type be guided automatically in flying
machines by wireless or other rays, without a human pilot,
in ceaseless procession upon a hostile city, arsenal, camp,
or dockyard?

———————◆———————

Although Churchill had no expertise in physics, he was not without instruction about the subject. One of his closest confidants and
a frequent guest at his country home, Chartwell, in the 1930s was
Frederick Lindemann, a physicist at Christ Church, Oxford. It was
Clementine Churchill who first brought him to the attention of her
husband; Lindemann was her sometime tennis partner. A physical
fitness advocate, the lean and ascetic Lindemann, who was both
vegetarian and a teetotaler, might not have been viewed as a likely
companion for Churchill. There was, however, a meeting of minds.
They shared a curiosity and imagination—and an eagerness to explore
new concepts. Lindemann—known as the "Prof" to his friends—
could transcend technical jargon and speak in the language of a lay-
man. The military historian John Keegan has described Lindemann
as having "an eclectic scientific mind and a brilliant gift of exposition,
precisely the qualities Churchill valued." At the dinner table at Chartwell, Churchill issued a challenge: "Prof, tell us in words of one

syllable, and in no longer than five minutes, what is the Quantum Theory." Churchill produced his gold pocket watch and began timing. Churchill led the applause when the Prof met the challenge.

Throughout the 1930s and World War II, Churchill relied on Lindemann for scientific advice, requesting his assistance to evaluate a wide range of concepts. Lindemann thought Churchill was an innate scientist and had missed his vocation. He later wrote of Churchill, "He has pre-eminently the synthetic mind which makes every new piece of knowledge fall into place and interlock with previous knowledge; where the ordinary brain is content to add each new experience to the scrap heap, he insists on fitting it into the structure of the cantilever jutting out over the abyss of ignorance."

Conversations with Lindemann no doubt contributed to the speculations that found their way into "Should We All Commit Suicide?" and other essays. After one of Lindemann's weekend visits, Churchill wrote asking, "My dear Lindemann, I have undertaken to write on the future possibilities of war and frightful it will be for the human race. On this subject, I have a good many ideas, but I should very much like to have another talk with you following on the most interesting one we had when you last touched here."

A prescient and wide-ranging essay from *The Strand* magazine, "Fifty Years Hence" (1931), explored the potential of nuclear power. Churchill made a number of predictions of future technology that have come to pass, such as wireless telephones, television, processed food, and robotics. "[T]he age we live in," Churchill wrote, "differs from all other ages in human annals.... What is it that has produced this new prodigious speed of man? Science is the cause."

About nuclear power, he discerned the concept of energy density that is the key to nuclear power and nuclear weapons alike. And he went beyond nuclear fission to outline the future of fusion power too:

> Nuclear energy is incomparably greater than the molecular
> energy which we use today. The coal a man can get in a day

can easily do five hundred times as much work as the man himself. Nuclear energy is at least one million times more powerful still. If the hydrogen atoms in a pound of water could be prevailed upon to combine together and form helium, they would suffice to drive a thousand-horsepower engine for a whole year. If the electrons, those tiny planets of the atomic systems, were induced to combine with the nuclei in the hydrogen the horsepower liberated would be 120 times greater still. There is no question among scientists that this gigantic source of energy exists. What is lacking is the match to set the bonfire alight, or it may be the detonator to cause the dynamite to explode. The Scientists are looking for this.

One can see in this and similar passages how Churchill's genuine fascination with science and technology went hand in hand with his sober appreciation of their potential for catastrophe: "And with the hopes and powers [of progress] will come dangers out of all proportion to the growth of man's intellect, to the strength of his character or to the efficacy of his institutions."

In particular, Churchill worried that "the modern commander [will be] entirely divorced from the heroic aspect by the physical conditions which have overwhelmed his art." With future wars likely to be directed by push-button commanders far from the battlefield, "there will not be much glory for the General in this process." Churchill compares military leaders of the new era to his gardener exterminating a wasps' nest—despite his technological effectiveness, "I am not going to regard him as a hero."

Churchill was alert to the ominous possibility that "the possession by one side of some overwhelming scientific advantage would lead to the complete enslavement of the unwary party." When the United States became the first nation to develop nuclear weapons, Churchill was greatly relieved. In 1948 he remarked, "What do you suppose would be the position this afternoon had it been Communist Russia instead of free enterprise America which had created the atomic weapon? Instead of being a somber guarantee of peace it would have become an irresistible method of human enslavement."

Once the Soviet Union matched the United States and its allies in nuclear technology, Churchill repeated his admonition from the years after World War I—that the awful prospect of nuclear war "should make the prevention of another great war the main preoccupation of mankind." As we shall see in a later chapter, Churchill's Cold War statesmanship was ahead of its time but was ultimately vindicated. At its core, however, was his uneasy acceptance of the nuclear balance of terror.

In his last major speech to the House of Commons as prime minister, in 1955, Churchill dwelt at length on the threat of nuclear annihilation. He recalled his 1931 article predicting the development of nuclear power but added that with the development of the even more powerful hydrogen bomb, "the entire foundation of human affairs was revolutionized, and mankind placed in a situation both measureless and laden with doom." And yet a full decade before formal deterrence doctrines became the cornerstone of American and NATO policy, Churchill explained the terrible logic that he thought provided the best chance to avoid the destruction of the human race:

> [A] curious paradox has emerged. Let me put it simply. After a certain point has been passed it may be said, "The worse things get, the better." ... Then it may well be that we shall by a process of sublime irony have reached a stage in this story where safety will be the sturdy child of terror, and survival the twin brother of annihilation.

The strategy of deterrence, he went on to argue, required "patience and courage." In a speech to a joint session of Congress on one of his last visits to the United States, Churchill said, "Be careful above all things not to let go of the atomic weapon until you are sure and more than sure that other means of preserving peace are in your hands!"

The day might come, he hoped, when the world would emerge from the nuclear shadow. That day has not come, and never will, but with the end of the Cold War we are certainly better off than we were in the decades when two nations stood poised to destroy each other in a half hour with a hail of thousands of nuclear warheads. Churchill's advice today would surely be the same as in 1955: "Meanwhile, never flinch, never weary, never despair."

CHAPTER 8

THE MODERN OIL CRISIS PREDICTED

CHURCHILL CAUTIONS AGAINST FOREIGN OIL DEPENDENCE

"Energy crisis" did not enter our vocabulary until the 1970s, when the oil-producing nations of the Middle East began colluding to charge high prices for crude oil. The cost squeeze, like a gun aimed at our head, compelled us to examine our energy practices and explore other sources of fuel more intensely. We could have found a warning of this predicament from Churchill if we had looked back far enough.

When Churchill arrived at the Admiralty in 1911 and considered the prospect of an accelerating naval arms race with Germany, he concluded that the next generation of British warships needed two things—bigger guns and faster ships. Gun design advanced steadily, though Churchill pressed to leapfrog from the planned 13.5-inch guns to a 15-inch gun in new battleships. That increase in the barrel's diameter would almost double the weight of the shell that could be fired.

Building faster ships, however, was a matter of more than just design change. It would require converting the fleet's fuel supply from coal to oil. Churchill explained the strategic and tactical calculations that went into his thinking in a remarkable chapter in *The World Crisis* that bore the typically Churchillian title "The Romance of Design." Boosting the speed of frontline "Fast Division" ships from twenty-one knots to twenty-five or twenty-six—the speed he thought necessary to assure supremacy over the German fleet—would require installing additional boilers. The problem was where to put them. Adding the necessary boilers would require eliminating some gun turrets and increasing the amount of coal that ships would have to store and manage under steam, an unappealing and uneconomical prospect.

The superiority of oil-fired ships over coal-burning steamers was impressive. "The use of oil made it possible in every type of vessel to have more gun-power and more speed for less size and cost," Churchill argued. But there was a catch: while England was rich in coal, "oil was not found in appreciable quantities in our islands." The oil riches of the North Sea were unknown at the time and decades away from development. In the meantime, Churchill worried, "If we required it we must carry it by sea in peace or war from distant countries.... The oil supplies of the world were in the hands of vast oil trusts under foreign control. To commit the Navy irrevocably to oil was indeed 'to take arms against a sea of troubles.'"

After assessing the many formidable difficulties, Churchill nevertheless came down squarely in favor of oil: "If we overcame the difficulties and surmounted the risks... mastery itself was the prize of the venture." It was this phrase that inspired the energy expert Daniel Yergin to title his 1991 Pulitzer-winning book *The Prize*: "With that, Churchill, on the eve of World War I, had captured a fundamental truth, and one applicable not only to the conflagration that followed, but to the many decades ahead. For oil has meant mastery through the years since."

Securing an oil supply for future decades required Britain to forge the Anglo-Persian Oil agreement, which involved substantial British (and later American) investment in developing Middle Eastern oil fields. Beyond the direct investments, Britain and later the U.S. became vitally involved in the question of Middle Eastern stability. As colonial secretary after World War I, Churchill was closely involved with the dissolution of the Ottoman Empire and the emergence of the various nations of Iraq, Saudi Arabia, Kuwait, and so forth that transfix our attention today. Most of these nations emerged from the Cairo Treaty of 1922, the formation of which Churchill oversaw.

Britain's potential vulnerability to changes in the world oil market were prominent in his mind when he was chancellor of the exchequer in the 1920s, in part because he understood that global demand for oil would eventually soar. In one of his speeches during his chancellorship, Churchill observed that the automobile, which was a luxury item for the rich before the war, was developing into a necessity.

Even then the native populations of the Middle East were restive and fractious. The presence of royal troops in Egypt under the British Mandate stirred up continuing protests. Egypt was the largest Arab nation, and Cairo, its largest capital, was a breeding place for foes of Western domination. Egypt was asserting its claims on the Sudan, which bordered the Nile, the route to India via the Suez Canal. Churchill perceived that the hungry masses of the Middle East would be a ripe target for any despot who wanted to exploit Arab nationalism, Islamic extremism, and Marxist class hatred. Such tyrants could turn Britain's dependence on oil into extortion.

For all these reasons, Churchill warned in a newspaper column in July 1929:

> We used to be a source of fuel; we are increasingly becoming a sink. These suppliers of foreign liquid fuel are no doubt

vital to our industry, but our ever increasing dependence on them ought to arouse serious and timely reflections. The scientific utilization by liquefication, pulverization, and other processes of our vast and magnificent deposits of oil constitutes an objective of prime importance.

Once again, Churchill's prophetic insight anticipated what would become a central problem for leaders in our age.

PART III

DOMESTIC AFFAIRS

CHAPTER 9

A BALANCE BETWEEN CAPITALISM AND SOCIALISM

CHURCHILL'S SOLUTION OF A SOCIAL SAFETY NET

C hurchill has always been known primarily as a war leader, but he began his political career as a social reformer. He devoted most of his attention and energy before and between the two world wars to social and economic reform. His official biographer, Martin Gilbert, summarizes, "Both in his Liberal and Conservative years, Churchill was a radical; a believer in the need for the State to take an active part, both by legislation and finance, in ensuring minimum standards of life, labour and social well-being for all citizens."[1] And even though he spent most of his life as a member and leader of the Conservative (Tory) Party, very late in life (at age eighty-seven, in fact) he remarked to a new Labour member of Parliament, "I'm a Liberal; always have been."[2]

In his first decade in politics, Churchill was the sponsor or champion of a series of social reform measures, including the minimum wage, disability insurance, and maximum-hour laws. Later, as president of the Board of Trade, he expanded his agenda to include unemployment insurance and labor exchanges, which he thought would enhance the dynamism of labor markets and reduce unemployment. Churchill sympathized with the early-twentieth-century Progressive movement in the United States, which advocated similar measures and anticipated some features of Franklin Roosevelt's New Deal. Churchill admired both Roosevelt and the New Deal, and while Churchill has often been praised—or criticized—for being one of the early architects of the British welfare state, he also foresaw many of the serious defects of the welfare state with which we are so familiar and about which we are acutely concerned today. A close look at Churchill's careful views on social and economic questions shows both his prophetic foresight and his moderation—qualities that would be useful today as industrialized nations confront the crisis of an over-extended welfare state.

Churchill regarded the material advances of late-nineteenth-century industrialization as a great blessing, but he did not avert his gaze from the tradeoffs involved, such as the poor housing and working conditions of the rising working class. As a child of the upper class, Churchill had little firsthand experience observing poverty in Britain. He had grown up in another world—a world of stately country homes and fashionable townhouses, where the art of conversation and the manners of society were exquisitely practiced by gracious families, unburdened by the drudgery and chores of household care. These were people who had the time to read, talk, and discuss current affairs and fashion. As Churchill once said, "It was the world of the few and they were the very few."

The first time Churchill ever saw the face of poverty was at the time of his campaign for the parliamentary seat in Manchester.

Strolling out from his hotel headquarters one evening with his administrative secretary, Edward Marsh, he wandered among the grimy tenements of the slums. "Fancy," remarked Churchill to Marsh, "living in one of those streets—never seeing anything beautiful, never eating anything savory, never saying anything clever." An entirely new world, which he knew before only from reports and statistics, revealed its ugly face.

In his first year in the House of Commons, Churchill acquainted himself with some of the leading studies of urban poverty of his time, especially Seebohm Rowntree's recent book, *Poverty: A Study of Town Life* (1901), which contained a graphic account of the life of the poor in the city of York. In an early speech, Churchill said that Rowntree's book "has fairly made my hair stand on end." In a letter to a friend, Churchill expanded on the effect Rowntree's book had on him: "For my own part, I see little glory in an Empire which can rule the waves but is unable to flush its sewers.... What is wanted is a well-balanced policy midway between the Hotel Cecil and Exeter Hall, something that will coordinate development and expansion with the progress of social comfort and health." He went on to warn that "extremists on both sides" would make a moderate policy difficult to achieve. In other words, Churchill rejected both the socialists who prescribed redistribution or revolution, and the pure laissez-faire school that disdained any government measures to ameliorate poverty or the insecurity of the working classes. Churchill understood that the failure to ameliorate the worst conditions of poverty and the laboring classes would make socialist revolution *more* likely and that moderate social welfare measures would strengthen a market economy. As the historian Kenneth Morgan puts it, Churchill stood for "free enterprise with a human face."

Churchill's moderate approach emphasized not social revolution, but social insurance; not nationalization of industry, but regulation of industry. In 1906, this grandson of a duke explained how his agenda of unemployment insurance, a minimum wage, and the eight-hour day should be understood: "I do not want to see impaired the vigour of competition, but we can do much to mitigate the consequences of failure. We want to draw a line below which we will not allow persons to live and labour, yet above which they can compete with all the strength of their manhood." Speaking about eight-hour-workday laws, Churchill said:

> The general march of industry is not towards inadequate hours of work, but towards sufficient hours of leisure. People are not content that their lives should remain alternations between bed and factory; they demand time to look about them, time to see their houses by daylight, to see their children. Time to think and read and cultivate their gardens; time, in short, to live.

He later added old-age pensions, prison reform, and labor arbitration laws to his social reform agenda. He wanted to "spread a net over the abyss."

Churchill's understanding of a runaway welfare state's defects is clear in his reaction to a famous American book of the time, Upton Sinclair's *The Jungle*. Churchill found *The Jungle*, like Rowntree's book, a "really excellent and valuable piece of work" that "pierces the thickest skull and the most leathery heart. It forces people who never think about the foundations of society to pause and wonder." But in his rejection of Sinclair's remedy, socialist revolution, Churchill explained that socialism could never replace the most important ingredient of social welfare—human virtue:

> I must frankly say that if the conditions of society in Chicago are such as Mr. Upton Sinclair depicts, no mere economic revolution would in itself suffice to purify and

ennoble. A National or Municipal Beef Trust, with the United States Treasury at its back, might indeed give more regular employment at higher wages to its servants, and might sell cleaner food to its customers—at a price. But if evil systems corrupt good men, it is no less true that base men will dishonor any system, and while no bond of duty more exacting than that of material recompense regulates the relations of man and man, while no notion more lofty than self-interest animates the exertions of every class, and no hope beyond the limits of this fleeting world lights the struggles of humanity, the most admirable systems will merely succeed in transferring, under different forms and pretexts, the burden of toil, misery, and injustice from one set of human shoulders to another.

Even before they became partners in prosecuting World War II, Churchill admired Franklin Delano Roosevelt. In a famous essay about Roosevelt published in 1937, Churchill observed that "the courage, the power and the scale of his effort must enlist the ardent sympathy of every country, and his success could not fail to lift the whole world forward into the sunlight of an easier and more genial age." He added that "in truth Roosevelt is an explorer who has embarked on a voyage as uncertain as that of Columbus and upon a quest which might conceivably be as important as the discovery of the New World."

One of Roosevelt's closest political advisers, Thomas ("the Cork") Corcoran, told Churchill that Churchill's early workmen's compensation, unemployment compensation, and pension programs "were the models of those of us who drafted those Depression bills." But like his evaluation of Upton Sinclair's socialist prescriptions in *The Jungle*, Churchill's essay about Roosevelt sounded valuable cautions about the limits and defects of the New Deal—warnings that have been borne out by subsequent historical scholarship. The economic emergency of the Great Depression had created the conditions of a virtual dictatorship by FDR, and "[a]lthough the Dictatorship is veiled by constitutional forms, it is nonetheless effective." While "the Roosevelt adventure claims sympathy and admiration from all of those in England," Churchill worried that "very considerable misgivings must necessarily arise when a campaign to attack the monetary problem becomes intermingled with, and hampered by, the elaborate processes of social reform and the struggles of class warfare." Specifically, Churchill feared that Roosevelt's pro-union policies would drive labor unions to the Left. In Britain, he noted, extreme and intransigent trade unionism "has introduced a narrowing element into our public life. It has been a keenly-felt impediment to our productive and competitive power."

Related to this was Churchill's criticism of Roosevelt's "disposition to hunt down rich men as if they were noxious beasts." In language that could be applied to President Barack Obama's so-called "Buffett Rule," Churchill wrote, "The question arises whether the general well-being of the masses of the community will be advanced by an excessive indulgence in this amusement.... To hunt wealth is not to capture commonwealth."

In the run-up to his second premiership after World War II, Churchill warned against the endless expansion of the welfare state that had become the credo of the Labour Party. In 1949, while still in opposition, he sounded the cry for fiscal restraint: "We are not going to try to get into office by offering bribes and promises of immediate material benefit to our people.... It would be far better for us to lose the election than to win it on false pretense." It is unfortunate that modern politicians do not follow this prophetic example of Churchill's as well.

CHAPTER 10

UNMASKING SOCIALISM

CHURCHILL ANTICIPATES ITS FAILURE

C hurchill formed and deepened his social and economic views at a time when socialism of every variety was on the rise and said to be the "wave of the future." In the first decades of the twentieth century, Churchill came in close contact with at least three varieties of socialism: the "Fabian" socialism of Sidney and Beatrice Webb, Bernard Shaw, and others; the revolutionary socialism of the more extreme trade unions that was indistinguishable from Marxist Communism; and still another hybrid strain that stopped short of full state ownership but emphasized centralized economic planning. This third strain formed the basis for the nationalistic fascisms of the inter-war period. Churchill rejected them all. His most famous formulation on the subject was his comment from 1945: "The inherent vice of Capitalism is the unequal sharing of blessings. The inherent virtue of Socialism is the equal sharing of miseries."

Churchill was hardly the earliest to denounce socialism. Yet he was the first statesman with reformist credentials to articulate why state socialism was a recipe for economic disaster. In those prewar years, Churchill, strangely, was denounced as a "socialist" by many members of the House of Lords—colleagues of his cousin, the duke of Marlborough. But Churchill always saw through socialism's pernicious promise. He perceived not only that collectivism would destroy private enterprise but that the totalitarian power its practitioners sought would strangle economic growth and could only end in failure.

It is still today a popular mistake in political discourse to blur the lines between liberalism (of the classical and reformist kind that Churchill embraced) and socialism. Churchill understood the difference, as marked in one of his memorable speeches at Kinnaird Hall to his constituency in Dundee in May 1908:

> Liberalism is not Socialism, and will never be. There is a great gulf fixed. It is not only a gulf of method, it is a gulf of principle... Socialism wants to pull down wealth. Liberalism seeks to raise up poverty. Socialism would destroy private interests. Liberalism would preserve them in the only way they can be preserved, by reconciling them with public right. Socialism seeks to kill enterprise. Liberalism seeks to rescue enterprise from the trammels of privilege and preference. Socialism assails the preeminence of the individual. Liberalism seeks to build up the minimum standard of the masses. Socialism attacks capital. Liberalism attacks monopoly.

Churchill went on to say, "the Socialists have a creed of self-sacrifice but preach it in the language of spite, envy, hatred, and uncharitableness." Churchill then mused on the "barrenness of a philosophy whose creed was absolute collectivism" and the "equality of reward irrespective of services rendered." Churchill regarded the slogan, "from each according to his ability, to each according to his need" as tantamount to "you shall work according to your fancy, you shall be paid according to your appetite."

In the 1920s there emerged among a handful of renegade economists such as Ludwig von Mises and F. A. Hayek (who later won the Nobel Prize in economics) an awareness of the inherent defects of socialist economic planning. The nub of their critique was that a "command" economy without freely set market prices would founder quickly by misallocating resources. Decades later, even Communist countries would come to see the truth of this insight. What is uncanny is how fully Churchill anticipated these arguments two decades before academic economists first made them. In a March 1908 speech, Churchill anticipated in broad strokes what Hayek would explain more fully in his classic 1945 essay "The Use of Knowledge in Society." As Churchill put it:

> I reject as impracticable the insane Socialist idea that we could have a system whereby the whole national production of the country, with all its infinite ramifications, should be organized and directed by a permanent official, however able, from some central office. The idea is not only impossible, but unthinkable. If it was even attempted it would produce a most terrible shrinkage and destruction of productive energy.

At one point Churchill wanted to write a book about socialism to be called *The Creed of Failure*. He outlined the first five chapters, and even though he was one of the bestselling authors of his age, so strong was the enthusiasm for socialism that he could not find a publisher and had to abandon the idea.

Churchill was more directly involved in economic policy in the 1920s, when he served as chancellor of the exchequer. During these years he came to oppose economic planning and interventionist schemes that, while falling short of complete socialism, partook of some of the same planning fallacies inherent to socialism.

In 1929, at the outset of the Great Depression, Churchill opposed a proposal for a government-funded jobs program. John Maynard Keynes had just co-authored a book, *We Can Conquer Unemployment*, advocating deficit spending to stimulate the economy—a prelude to his *General Theory of Employment, Interest, and Money*, which became the cornerstone of "Keynesianism."

Churchill's argument against the jobs scheme foreshadowed all of the criticisms that would be directed against Keynesian-style spending programs, down to the "stimulus" program of President Obama. In a speech to the House, Churchill noted that the government already borrowed money for necessary public works projects, but that "for the purposes of curing unemployment the results have certainly been meager. They are, in fact, so meager as to lend considerable color to the orthodox Treasury doctrine which has steadfastly held that, whatever might be the political or social advantages, very little additional employment and no permanent additional employment can in fact and as a general rule be created by State borrowing and State expenditure."

As Churchill approached the 1945 general election, held shortly after the war in Europe had been won, the Conservative Party embraced Hayek's recent bestselling book, *The Road to Serfdom*. (The Conservative Party wanted to distribute a condensed version of Hayek's book as a campaign piece, but could not get the paper—still under wartime rationing—to print the tract.) The book inspired Churchill to give one of his most infamous denunciations of socialism. "No Socialist system can be established without a political police. Many of those who are advocating Socialism or voting Socialist today will be horrified at this idea. That is because they are short-sighted, that is because they do not see where their theories are leading them." Churchill should have stopped right there. But he went on to suggest the extreme consequences of socialist policy: there would be "some form of Gestapo" which would "gather all the power to the supreme party and the party leaders, rising like stately pinnacles above their vast bureaucracies of Civil servants, no longer servants and no longer civil." Churchill's use of the term "Gestapo" in connection with his former coalition partners from the Labour Party went down very poorly with British voters. Churchill's wife and several close colleagues had urged him to remove the Gestapo reference, but he refused. His extreme language is thought to have contributed to the landslide loss his party suffered in the July 1945 election.

Hayek wrote to the historian Paul Addison, "I am afraid there can be little doubt that Winston Churchill's somewhat unfortunately phrased Gestapo speech was written under the influence of *The Road to Serfdom.*" Meeting Hayek briefly a few years later, Churchill indicated his familiarity with the book but told Hayek "it would never happen in England"—a view Hayek himself embraced in his later books.

Churchill did not back away from his embrace of Hayek's critique of socialist-style policies. While the leader of the opposition in 1947, Churchill opposed the socialist policies of the Attlee government that were leading to the progressive nationalization of basic industries in the following terms:

> When losses are made, under the present system those losses are borne by the individuals who sustained them and took the risk and judged things wrongly, whereas under State management all losses are quartered upon the taxpayers and the community as a whole. The elimination of the profit motive and of self-interest as a practical guide in the myriad transactions of daily life will restrict, paralyse and destroy British ingenuity, thrift, contrivance and good housekeeping at every stage in our life and production, and will reduce all our industries from a profit-making to a loss-making process.

Richard Langworth, editor of *Churchill by Himself: The Definitive Collection of Quotations*, said, "Churchill had been reading, and was deeply impressed by, the Austrian economist Friedrich Hayek's seminal book, *The Road to Serfdom*. This statement could have been made by Hayek himself."

In the 1970s and 1980s, Hayek's critique of socialism became widely accepted on both sides of the Iron Curtain, and Hayek was a favorite author of both Margaret Thatcher and Ronald Reagan. As in so many other cases, Churchill got there far ahead of everyone else.

CHAPTER II

POSTWAR TECHNOPHOBIA

CHURCHILLIAN ASSESSMENTS

As we saw in Churchill's prophecies about modern warfare, he anticipated the effect that rapidly advancing technology would have on warfare, especially on air power and nuclear weapons. But he also anticipated—and shared to a certain extent—the general public apprehension about technology that became widespread especially after World War II. The fear that technology would come to dominate or threaten human wellbeing was not a novelty of the twentieth century; it is at least as old as Mary Shelley's cautionary tale in *Frankenstein*. But the pace and scale of technological change in the twentieth century took technophobia to new heights. Most of the leading "anti-utopian" novels of the postwar years, such as George Orwell's *1984* and C. S. Lewis's *That Hideous Strength*, emphasize the role of science in enabling tyranny and dehumanizing society.

To Churchill, the advances in scientific technology were a mixed blessing—the improvements in daily life also increased the danger of intrusion into individual lives. As Churchill put it, "On the one hand, science opens up a chasm of self-destruction. On the other hand, she displays a vision of plenty and comfort." It was Churchill's appreciation of the potential benefit and misuse of modern science that led him to make one of his starkest warnings about the specter of a Nazi triumph. In his "Finest Hour" speech of 1940, Churchill said, "But if we fail, then the whole world, including the United States, including all that we have known and cared for, will sink into the abyss of a new Dark Age made more sinister, and perhaps more protracted, by the lights of perverted science." But he had worried about what he called "the sombre paths of destructive science" as early as 1925, long before Hitler and his perverted scientists arrived on the scene. In an early essay in which Churchill speculated about nuclear weapons and ballistic missiles, he wrote of "the march of Science unfolding ever more appalling possibilities."

Another of Churchill's uncanny feats of prophecy was an article first published in *Maclean's* in 1931 entitled "Fifty Years Hence," in which he anticipates television, mobile phones, and many other modern technological marvels that are now commonplace. "Wireless telephones and television," he predicted, "following naturally on their present path of development, would enable their owner to connect up with any room similarly installed, and hear and take part in the conversation as well as if he had put his head in through the window." As in his essay "Shall We All Commit Suicide?", Churchill worried about the political and social disruption technology might bring. He warned about the importance of subordinating technology to humankind's moral principles and purposes:

> It is therefore above all things important that the moral philosophy and spiritual conceptions of men and nations should hold their own amidst these formidable scientific

evolutions. It would be much better to call a halt in material progress and discovery rather than to be mastered by our own apparatus and the forces which it directs. There are secrets too mysterious for man in his present state to know; secrets which once penetrated may be fatal to human happiness and glory. But the busy hands of the scientists are already fumbling with the keys of all the chambers hitherto forbidden to mankind.

Churchill returned to this theme again and again. In the 1946 Iron Curtain speech he said, "The dark ages may return—the Stone Age may return on the gleaming wings of science."

It is fitting that Churchill returned to this theme in 1949 at a convocation address at the Massachusetts Institute of Technology, which he titled "The Twentieth Century: Its Promise and Its Realization." Churchill saluted the president of MIT for retaining an emphasis on teaching the humanities at a university known for its scientific and technical focus:

How right you are in this great institution of technical study and achievement to keep a Dean of Humanities and give him so commanding a part to play in your discussions! No technical knowledge can outweigh knowledge of the humanities in the gaining of which philosophy and history walk hand in hand. Our inheritance of well-founded, slowly conceived codes of honor, morals and manners, the passionate convictions which so many hundreds of millions share together of the principles of freedom and justice, are far more precious to us than anything which scientific discoveries could bestow. Those whose minds are attracted or compelled to rigid and symmetrical systems of government should remember that logic, like science, must be the servant and not the master of man.

With this lifelong concern in mind, it is not surprising that after his retirement from active politics, Churchill helped to establish Churchill College at Cambridge University in the late 1950s. The college was to emphasize science and technology, rather than politics or statesmanship as one might have expected, because Churchill was apprehensive that British scientists, unversed in history or the humanities, might conduct their future explorations or experiments in a moral vacuum. Churchill thought the world needed more scientists who had not been too narrowly confined to their technological fields without the breadth of more knowledge in history, philosophy, and the humanities. He saw specialization as the curse of the modern world. "We need scientists in the world but not a world of scientists," he said. The machine was not to be man's master but his servant.

In a rough sense, Churchill hoped his namesake college would be the British equivalent of MIT, meeting a need that the colleges of Oxford and Cambridge did not address. "Oxbridge" students specialized in a single field in their three years of undergraduate studies, typically reading "P. P. and E." (philosophy, politics, and economics), "Greats" (Greek, Latin, and Ancient History), modern languages, chemistry and biology, mathematics and physics, or other specialized disciplines.

Churchill disdained such narrowly trained scientists as one-dimensional technocrats and agreed with the sentiment of C. P. Snow, a physicist and novelist, who declared in a famous lecture, "The Two Cultures," "The scientist who does not understand Hamlet is as ignorant as the playwright who doesn't understand the theory of relativity."

Cambridge was commonly thought to be more open than Oxford to new concepts in science, so Churchill considered it the better setting in which to test his radical proposal for teaching the sciences. University students preparing for careers in nuclear physics or biochemistry would learn from respected historians, recognized economists, and other distinguished professors of the humanities and social sciences.

Almost as radical was Churchill's insistence that the new college be open to women as well as men. Although there were women's colleges in Oxford and Cambridge, Churchill was the first college in either university to accept women on an equal footing with men.

In January 1959, Churchill, as chairman of the college trustees, appointed Sir John Cockcroft, a Nobel laureate in physics, to be the first master of the college. Churchill had worked with him during his second term as prime minister and knew him to be that uncommon type of scientist who had read Toynbee and Gibbon and could quote T. S. Eliot as well as Shakespeare. This was the precedent Churchill wanted to establish for the masters of his college.

Although Churchill told students at MIT, "Science, no doubt, could, if sufficiently perverted, exterminate us all," he added that "On the whole I remain an optimist."

PART IV

THE AGE OF TOTALITARIAN IDEOLOGIES

CHAPTER 12

AN OMINOUS NOVEL

CHURCHILL IMAGINES A HITLER-LIKE FIGURE

One of Churchill's more remarkable but often forgotten achievements was winning the Nobel Prize for literature—rarely awarded for nonfiction—for his four-volume *History of the English-Speaking Peoples* in 1953. In the laureate's vast literary corpus there was a single novel, *Savrola*, written when he was just twenty-three years old. Though Churchill regarded this excursion into fiction as juvenilia—in later years he would warn friends away from reading the book—it depicted a Hitler-like figure more than twenty years before the rise of the fascist dictators. And displaying its youthful author's understanding of the power of oratory in a democratic age, the novel foreshadowed several aspects of Churchill's own role in opposing Hitler. With its depictions of the demagogic villain and his Churchillian nemesis, *Savrola* represents an extraordinary act of double-prophecy. Indeed, Robert Lewis Taylor, an early biographer of Churchill, wrote that *Savrola* "has since been characterized as one of the most dazzling pieces of unconscious personal prophecy on record."

Savrola is set in a mythical Balkan country called Laurania. (The Latin names of the characters suggest Romania.) The novel offers insight into Churchill's mind at the time he began his career as a soldier and journalist. The protagonist, Savrola, is a young soldier—a figure Churchill obviously modeled after himself—who turns into an activist and plots to overthrow a repressive regime.

The novel was not a critical success in its time, but contemporary judgments were shortsighted. *Savrola* contains serious teaching about political moderation and the use of political rhetoric—matters to which the young Churchill had already given serious thought. In a long, unpublished letter from India to his mother a year before *Savrola* was published, Churchill showed a deep understanding not only of the nature of successful political oratory, but its utility for an independent politician such as he would turn out to be: "Of all the talents bestowed on men," Churchill wrote, "none is so precious as the gift of oratory. He who enjoys it wields a power more durable than that of a great king. He is an independent force in the world. Abandoned by his party, betrayed by his friends, stripped of his offices, whoever can command this power is still formidable." One description of Savrola's actions sounds very much like the description of Churchill the prime minister's oratorical feats of 1940: "In that scene of confusion and indecision he looked magnificent. His very presence imparted a feeling of confidence to his followers."

Savrola confronts the dilemmas of a statesman—his instigation of a revolt against a dictator risks enabling a more extremist element to install an even worse regime. The main theme of the novel is how Savrola seeks to resolve this dilemma. There are personal stories along the way. Laurania's dictator, Antonio Molara, instructs his beautiful wife, Lucile, to insinuate herself into Savrola's confidence and learn what he could be planning. Readers with a Freudian bent might see in the romance that develops between Savrola and Lucile Churchill's own adulation of his lustrous mother and his ambivalence towards his father, Lord Randolph, who had coldly dismissed his son's ambitions.

But it was a secondary character in the Lauranian rebellion that made a minor sensation when Churchill's long-forgotten novel was republished in 1956, a year after he retired from government. In the world's eyes, the two leaders who personified the war between fascism and freedom were the Nazi Führer and the resolute British prime minister. *Savrola* depicts a German ex-corporal named Karl Kreutze, who eventually takes over the Nationalist and Socialist movement and becomes the dictator of Laurania.

Kreutze bears a strong resemblance to Hitler, who was in diapers when Churchill wrote his novel. Whether the creation of this character was a coincidence or clairvoyance or some combination of the two can only be determined by a closer look at the years just before the novel's composition.

In a five-month visit to Cuba early in his career (1895), when the island was trying to throw off the last vestiges of Spanish colonial rule, Churchill had witnessed rebellion against oppressive government. He had obtained a position with the Spanish army as a neutral military observer and then talked the *Daily Graphic* of London into making him their correspondent. In one dispatch, Churchill penned a telling remark: "I sympathize with the rebellion—not with the rebels." That attitude would color his views for the rest of his life.

For the first time, he sensed the heady appeal of nationalism and the hold its rhetoric had on the masses. He could also see the effect of the rebel leaders' socialist promises to the sugar cane workers and tobacco field crews. In *Savrola*, the "League" which spearheads the rebellion comprises members of the Nationalist and Socialist parties. The idealistic Savrola nonetheless worries about the tyranny and violence that might accompany "the political waves of a social tide that is flowing." The future, he says, "is inscrutable but appalling."

In Cuba the most appalling of the rebel insurrectionists was Maceo—a machete-wielding fanatic whose terror tactics brutalized the Spanish rulers. Maceo, who sometimes styled himself as "numero uno," may have been the model for Karl Kreutze, the leader of the Lauranian radicals. These violent militants, with their own rituals and paraphernalia, refer to Kreutze as "Number One." Savrola confides to a fellow reformist, "The secret society they call the League is an unknown factor. I hate that fellow, Kreutze, Number One as he styles himself… the Labour delegates all seem to be under his influence."

At the close of the novel, Molara surrenders to armed insurgents on the pledge that his life will be saved. Kreutze nevertheless steps up to Molara and shoots him in the head. Seeing the corpse of the president, Savrola asks, "Who has committed the murder?" "It is not a murder," replies Kreutze. "It is an execution." "By whose authority?" asks Savrola. "In the name of the Society," answers Kreutze. Churchill adds, in the voice of Savrola, that Karl Kreutze was a man of the people. His socialistic writings had been widely read as he was the head of the Secret Society.

A novelist can convey meaning through the names he gives his characters, as Dickens did with his Pecksniff and Scrooge. Might Karl Kreutze's Christian name have been a nod to Karl Marx? And was the surname Kreutze, which in German means "cross," meant to conjure up the fanatical zealot? It is interesting that the swastika, chosen as the emblem of the Nazis, appeared to Christians as a perversion and distortion of the cross.

Lucile is clearly modeled after Lady Randolph. Churchill himself suggests this when he reveals that Lucile's French nickname is

"Jeanette," the given name of Lady Randolph—Jeanette Jerome—and the name by which she was known in her circle of friends in Paris.

> As she stood in the clear light of the autumn evening, she looked divinely beautiful. She had arrived at the stage of life when to the attraction of a maiden's beauty are added those of a woman's wit.

Churchill continues, "Her salon was crowded with the most famous men from every country. Statesmen, soldiers, poets, and men of science had worshipped at her shrine."

Elsewhere in *Savrola*, Churchill offers thumbnail descriptions of men from the real world of politics around him. On British gunboat diplomacy: "They must keep things going abroad to divert the public mind from advanced legislation." Of the mindless professional soldier, similar to the many British generals for whom Churchill had contempt: "General Sorrento was one of those soldiers, not an uncommon type, who fear little but independent responsibility." Of the political fickleness of businessmen: "The idea of bombardment was repugnant to the fat burgesses who had joined the party of revolt as soon as it became obvious that it was the winning side." The novel also contains some of his famous philosophical aphorisms, such as "Civilization [is] a state of society where moral force begins to escape from the tyranny of physical forces."

Perhaps there is a third prophecy to be gleaned from *Savrola*. As he wrote to readers at the time of the book's publication, "I chose as a theme a revolt in some imaginary Balkan or South American republic and traced the fortunes of a liberal leader who overthrew an arbitrary government only to be swallowed up by a socialist revolution...." Some readers of the novel fancy its ending a prediction of Churchill's own defeat to Labour in 1945. Savrola has to flee the country to save himself and Lucile from death at the hands of the triumphant (for the time being) revolutionaries. Although the novel ends in political tragedy (foreshadowing the title of the last volume of Churchill's World War II memoirs—*Triumph and Tragedy*), there is a hint of a happy resolution beyond the last page:

> Those who care to follow further the annals of the Republic of Laurania may read how, after the tumults had subsided, the hearts of the people turned again to the illustrious exile who had won them freedom, and whom they had deserted in the hour of victory. They may, scoffing at the fickleness of men, read of the return of Savrola, and his beautiful consort, to the ancient city they had loved so well.

This passage suggests a sequel, which Churchill never wrote. It is found, instead, in his own life story.

CHAPTER 13

MISGIVINGS ABOUT THE MIDDLE EAST

CHURCHILL ANTICIPATES THE POTENTIAL FOR ISLAMIC TERRORISM

I n 2004, Winston Churchill II met President George W. Bush in the Oval Office and read his grandfather's 1921 speech to the House of Commons that predicted a terrorist threat posed by a fanatical sect of Islam—the Wahabis. The words of warning from the statesman who invented the modern nation of Iraq (and which he later pronounced to be "an ungrateful volcano") found an attentive listener in the American president.

Having encouraged the Arab tribes in the Middle East to take sides against the German-allied Turks in World War I, Britain felt itself to be responsible for sorting out the political chaos produced by the Ottoman Empire's demise. Churchill's speech on the problem bore a remarkable resemblance to the situation the Bush administration faced with its difficult and costly occupation of Iraq. Churchill's words might have been Bush's:

> We are at the moment in possession of these countries. We have destroyed the only other form of government that existed there. We have made promises that I have already recited to the inhabitants, and we must endeavour to do our duty, to behave in a sober and honourable manner, and to discharge the obligations which we entered into with our eyes open. We cannot repudiate light-heartedly these undertakings. We cannot turn around and march our armies hastily to the coast and leave the inhabitants, for whose safety and well-being we have made ourselves responsible in the most public and solemn manner, a prey to anarchy and confusion of the worst description.

In other words, although Churchill acknowledged that "the obligation is not an unlimited one," it was a moral duty, as well as a political necessity, to install a stable government in Baghdad. "We have no intention of forcing upon the people of Iraq a ruler who is not of their own choice."

While most of Churchill's address concerned his plans to reduce the enormous expense of maintaining the British garrison in the Middle East, he could not avoid addressing the "delicate" political and religious character of the region. Churchill was behind the installation of King Faisal of Syria as the ruler of Iraq, in preference to the house of Ibn Saud. France opposed Churchill's choice, for Faisal had led Syrian troops against the French during the war. Yet Churchill believed that this charismatic and intelligent second son of Hussein, the aged descendant of the Prophet, was the best choice to rule over the new state of Iraq. To Churchill, Faisal was not a fanatic. He would accept a monarchical role in the new Iraq, even if it meant allowing the return of Jews to Palestine.

But there was one reason above all for Churchill's preference of Faisal over Ibn Saud:

> The religious views with which [Ibn Saud] is identified, and which his followers would be bound to enforce, would, of course, have set the whole of Mesopotamia in a blaze.... A large number of Ibn Saud's followers belong to the Wahabi sect, a form of Mohammedanism which bears, roughly speaking, the same relation to orthodox Islam as the most militant form of Calvinism would have borne to Rome in the fiercest times of the religious wars. The Wahabis profess a life of exceeding austerity, and what they practice themselves they rigorously enforce on others. They hold it as an article of duty, as well as of faith, to kill all who do not share their opinions and to make slaves of their wives and children. Women have been put to death in Wahabi villages for simply appearing in the streets.... Austere, intolerant, well-armed, and bloodthirsty, in their own regions the Wahabis are a distinct factor which must be taken into account, and they have been, and still are, very dangerous....

The key phrase in this assessment is perhaps "in their own regions." Churchill was not unaware of the potential for Islamic extremism's spread beyond its native region and into a wider jihad against the Christian West. Churchill had experienced firsthand the fanaticism for jihad of an extreme Sunni sect when he rode in that last cavalry charge against the Dervishes in 1898. These soldiers for Islam saw death in battle as their ticket to paradise, and were characterized by their strident war cries and frenetic scimitar-wielding attacks.

Churchill feared the fanaticism he saw. Such eagerness to die for beliefs violated his sensibilities. He predicted in 1921, "As the horn is to the rhinoceros, the sting to the wasp, so Islam is to the Arab—a weapon of offense or defense." Such violent militancy, as practiced by the Wahabi sect, worried Churchill. It was like Puritanism carried to its most punitive extreme.

Churchill recorded a harsh judgment of fanatical Islam in the original, unabridged edition of *The River War* that he later suppressed for political reasons. The following politically incorrect passage does not appear in the subsequent editions:

> How dreadful are the curses which Mohammedanism lays on its votaries! Besides the fanatical frenzy, which is as dangerous in a man as hydrophobia in a dog, there is this fearful fatalistic apathy. The effects are apparent in many countries. Improvident habits, slovenly systems of agriculture, sluggish methods of commerce, and insecurity of property exist wherever the followers of the Prophet rule or live. A degraded sensualism deprives this life of its grace and refinement; the next of its dignity and sanctity. The fact that in Mohammedan law every woman must *belong* to some man as his absolute property—either as a child, a wife, or a concubine—must delay the final extinction of slavery until the faith of Islam has ceased to be a great power among men. Individual Moslems may show splendid qualities. Thousands become the brave and loyal soldiers of the Queen: all know how to die. But the influence of the religion paralyzes the social development of those who follow it. No stronger retrograde force exists in the world. Far from being moribund, Mohammedanism is a militant and proselytizing faith. It has already spread throughout Central Africa, raising fearless warriors at every step; and were it not that Christianity is sheltered in the strong arms of science—the science against which it had vainly struggled—the civilization of modern Europe might fall, as fell the civilization of ancient Rome.

Churchill's misgivings about Islam have been justified with a vengeance by the present-day Islamic terrorist quest to develop and deploy weapons of mass destruction against the infidel West.

The passage of a century has not dimmed the fanaticism of Islamic extremism, and while Churchill could not have foreseen the events of September 11, 2001, the response was a rough parallel to the decision of Britain to avenge the killing of General Charles Gordon by going to war against the Dervishes and their leader, the Mahdi, in the Sudan in 1898. Like Osama bin Laden's crusade to drive the American infidels from the Middle East, the Mahdi saw his sacking of Khartoum in 1885 as the beginning of a jihad to purge all Egypt of the European infidels. Churchill's description of Britain's grim determination recalls for a reader today the exhausted patience and dissatisfaction with the mere "stability" of post-9/11 America:

> No terms but fight or death were offered. No reparation or apology could be made.... The red light of retribution played on the bayonets and the lances, and civilization— elsewhere sympathetic, merciful, tolerant, ready to discuss or to argue, eager to avoid violence, to submit to law, to effect a compromise—here advanced with an expression of inexorable sternness, and rejecting all other courses, offered only the arbitration of the sword.

CHAPTER 14

"IT IS NOT A CREED; IT IS A PESTILENCE"

CHURCHILL RECOGNIZES THE MENACE OF COMMUNISM

Winston Churchill was among the first statesmen to recognize the global malignity of Communism. In the pantheon of anti-Communists, from the Boshevik Revolution to the fall of the Berlin Wall, there are few who matched Churchill in denouncing the doctrine which he regarded as "a pestilence more destructive of life than the Black Death or the Spotted Typhus."

From the Communist Revolution's inception in 1917, Churchill abominated its architect, Vladimir Lenin, the dictator of the Soviet Union. Churchill described him as "implacable vengeance rising from a frozen pity. His sympathies as cold and wide as the Arctic Ocean; his hatreds tight as the hangman's noose. His purpose to save the world; his method to blow it up."[1] Noting one of history's ironies, Churchill said in the House of Commons, "It is with a sense of awe that [the Germans] turned upon Russia the most grisly of all weapons: Lenin."

In 1919, Churchill was prepared to send an army into Russia to strangle the infant Bolshevism in its cradle before it grew into monstrous adulthood. He was, at the time, secretary of state for munitions and supplies in the wartime coalition cabinet of David Lloyd George. Though Britain and America were united in their desire to crush Bolshevism in the waning months of the war with Germany, the idea of dispatching war-weary troops to the Russian interior to bolster the White army had little appeal. Churchill nonetheless warned the British of "the poison peril." "Russia," he said, "is being rapidly reduced by the Bolsheviks to an animal form of barbarism.... The Bolsheviks maintain themselves by bloody and wholesale butcheries.... Civilization is being completely extinguished over a gigantic area while Bolsheviks hop and caper like troops of ferocious baboons amid the ruins of cities and corpses of their victims."

His designs were stymied by a war-weary cabinet. Prime Minister Lloyd George was exasperated by Churchill's hawkishness. He told his fellow Liberal Sir George Riddell, "Winston... wants to conduct a war against the Bolsheviks. That would cause a revolution!" The press, conjuring up memories of Churchill and the Dardanelles, inveighed against "Mr. Churchill's War." With a heavy heart, Churchill, under orders from Lloyd George and the war cabinet, ordered the evacuation of the remaining British troops in Russia.

Despite his rebuff by Lloyd George and his cabinet colleagues, Churchill did not relent in his opposition to the Soviet Union. "I will always advocate... the overthrow and destruction of that criminal regime," Churchill said in 1920. He understood that revolutionary Communism bore a radically different character than garden variety socialism, which merely demanded government ownership of industry and central planning of the economy. He perceived that Communism was a revolutionary *faith*, promising not just material advance but the redemption and transformation of human nature itself. "Communism," said Churchill, "is a religion—Jesuits without Jesus." Communism's universalistic and international ambitions would destabilize other nations. "The Bolshevik," he said, "is not an idealist who is content to promote his cause by argument or example."

"Bolshevism is not a policy; it is a disease," Churchill told the House in 1920. "It is not a creed; it is a pestilence. It presents all the characteristics of a pestilence. It breaks out with great suddenness; it is violently contagious; it throws people into a frenzy of excitement; it spreads with extraordinary rapidity; the mortality is terrible; so that, after a while, like other pestilences, the disease tends to wear itself out."

This last comment is telling. Churchill recognized early on that Communism would ultimately fail because "it is fundamentally opposed to the needs and dictates of the human heart, and of human nature itself." In *Thoughts and Adventures* he elaborated:

> There is not one single social or economic principle or concept in the philosophy of the Russian Bolshevik which has not been realized, carried into action, and enshrined in immutable laws a million years ago by the White Ant. But human nature is more intractable than ant nature. The explosive variations of its phenomena disturb the smooth working out of the laws and forces which have subjugated the White Ant. It is at once the safeguard and the glory of mankind that they are easy to lead and hard to drive. So the Bolsheviks, having attempted by tyranny and by terror to establish the most complete form of mass life and collectivism of which history bears record, have not only lost the distinction of individuals, but have not even made the nationalization of life and industry pay. We have not much to learn from them, except what to avoid.

Even before Churchill trained his sights on Hitler and the Nazi menace, he foresaw the outline of the Cold War to come. During a visit
to America in 1931, he had announced confidently that "the two great
opposing forces of the future will be the English-speaking peoples and
Communism." While Churchill was ultimately confident that Soviet
Communism could not succeed, he knew that, like Nazism, it could
wreak untold havoc on the world before it expired. In winding up the
Russian operation in 1919, Churchill warned in a final memorandum:
"I do not believe any real harmony is possible with Bolshevism and
present civilization." He added, "The day will come when it will be
recognized without doubt throughout the civilized world that the
strangling of Bolshevism at birth would have been an untold blessing
to the human race."

CHAPTER 15

A LATTER-DAY MOSES

CHURCHILL PREDICTS THE FOUNDING
OF A JEWISH STATE IN PALESTINE

I n 1905, Winston Churchill envisioned the founding of a Jewish state in Palestine. He was the first elected politician to do this, twelve years before the Balfour Declaration, which promised British support for the Zionist plan to create a Jewish national home on the shores of the Mediterranean. While the Balfour Declaration was a wartime expedient to spur Jewish resistance to the Ottoman rulers in Palestine, Churchill's philo-Semitism was genuine.

Churchill was an ardent friend of leading Jews in Britain and a supporter of Zionism, expressing as early as 1908 his sympathy for a "restoration" of a Jewish homeland in Palestine. He successfully opposed an Aliens Bill brought to the House of Commons in 1904 that would have sharply restricted Jewish immigration into Britain. Only a month before the parliamentary debate on the bill, a congress of Jews meeting in Switzerland under the leadership of Theodor Herzl had rejected an offer by the British government for a homeland in Uganda, East Africa. They stuck to their dream of return and resettlement in Palestine. During the debate on the Aliens Bill, Churchill made known his sympathy for Zionism and ended his remarks saying, "I recognize the supreme attraction to a scattered people of a safe and settled home under a flag of tolerance and freedom. Such a plan contains a soul.... I do not feel that this noble vision ought to be allowed to fade, and I will do what I can to preserve and fill it."

Cheers rose from the Jews in the audience, and the British Jewish community promptly fell in line behind Churchill, as if he were a kind of latter-day Moses. One of their leaders rose at an all-Jewish meeting and announced that "any Jew who votes against Winston Churchill is a traitor to the common cause."

Later, as colonial secretary in the 1920s, Churchill took steps that enabled three hundred thousand Jews to emigrate to Palestine over the next decade, providing the nucleus for the future nation of Israel, and as prime minister in 1941 he proclaimed, "I was one of the authors" of Zionist policy. Indeed, among the lengthy catalogue of criticisms of Churchill was that "He was too fond of Jews."

Churchill's interest and sympathy for Jews was no matter of mere political opportunism. If anything, there was more of a negative political risk for Churchill. Anti-Semitism was still common in Edwardian England. Jews were barred from Oxford and Cambridge, as well as from Sandhurst. The only profession Jews could enter was the law. In society, Jews were not accepted at the races at Ascot or the regattas at Cowes. But Churchill was raised in a household where disparagement of Jews was not heard. One of Lord Randolph Churchill's political inspirations was Disraeli, and Lord Rothschild was a close and intimate friend of Churchill's mother, Jennie, after her husband's death. Rothschild even offered to take her son into his merchant bank if he failed admittance to Sandhurst.

Churchill's philo-Semitism had philosophical and cultural roots. In the fifth volume of his World War II memoirs, Churchill notes, "No two cities have counted more with mankind than Athens and Jerusalem. Their messages in religion, philosophy, and art have been the main guiding lights of modern faith and culture." As early as 1921, while visiting Jerusalem, Churchill commented, "We owe to the Jews in the Christian revelation a system of ethics which, even if it were entirely separated from the supernatural, would be incomparably the most precious possession of mankind, worth in fact the fruits of all other wisdom and learning put together. On that system and by that faith there has been built out of the wreck of the Roman Empire the whole of our existing civilization." The story of Moses, including the exodus through the parted Red Sea, should be taken literally, Churchill wrote in a remarkable essay in 1931. Moses was "one of the greatest human beings" who is to be associated with "the most decisive leap forward ever discernable in the human story." The Mosaic establishment of monotheism was "an idea of which all the genius of Greece and the power of Rome were incapable." Like all of Churchill's other historical speculations, this was not mere antiquarianism. He liked to repeat a saying attributed to Disraeli, "The Lord deals with the nations as the nations deal with the Jews."

The trickle of immigration into Palestine turned into a flood in the 1930s, the time of Hitler, and later during the Stalinist military occupation of Eastern Europe. Churchill saw the establishment of a Jewish state in Palestine as one of his prime postwar tasks, but one which had to wait until the war against Hitler was won, to the great frustration of David Ben-Gurion and other Zionists. Churchill's defeat in the 1945 election frustrated his design to see the establishment of a Jewish state fulfilled on his watch.

When Jews arose to fight for independence against the rule of the British Mandate, the Attlee government in 1948 dispatched troops to meet the resistance. Churchill, now out of power, spoke out against the British occupation and for the recognition of the new nation. The state of Israel was ultimately established, vindicating Churchill's vision. That the Jews had no greater friend in Britain than Churchill is evidenced by the sentiment a Jewish prisoner of war in a Soviet labor camp expressed during World War II, and which Martin Gilbert related: "We have no bread, but we have Churchill."

CHAPTER 16

THE INDIAN GENOCIDE PREDICTED

CHURCHILL'S WARNINGS ARE IGNORED AT GREAT COST

F ew episodes in Churchill's long career have attracted more critical commentary than his opposition to independence for India in the early 1930s. Most of this criticism, even from otherwise sympathetic observers, is inaccurate and unfair. The subsequent history of the subcontinent, much of which Churchill predicted, has confirmed many of his reasons for caution about Indian independence, even though he might have been surprised to see India become the world's largest democracy. Churchill might have been mistaken about the prospects for the success of self-government in India, but he was right in his main prediction that if India was prematurely granted independence, millions would be killed in religious riots and ethnic strife.

Much of the misperception and mischaracterization of Churchill's views on India derive from the superficial and simple-minded ideology of anti-colonialism that became popular after World War II, when the economically prostrate European powers moved to liquidate their remaining colonial territories as quickly as possible. It is supposed that Churchill's opposition to the government's 1930 bill to grant "dominion status" to India—the first step to complete independence—arose from his attachment to imperialism, from his reactionary paternalism. The only reason the term "racist" was not applied to him was because the word was not in use at that time. Churchill thought granting dominion status was premature; he was not opposed to eventual Indian self-government. In his weekly column in the *Daily Mail*, Churchill wrote, "The rescue of India, from the ages of barbarism, internecine war and tyranny, its slow but ceaseless forward march to civilization [was], upon the whole, the finest achievement of history."

In fact, Churchill was quite prepared to accept provincial self-government in India, provided Britain retained certain "rights of paramountcy," which meant control of foreign affairs and defense. Moreover, Churchill regarded the obligations of British rule in India as a matter of stewardship rather than perpetual control or exploitation. In a speech in August 1930 that most historians ignore, Churchill set out his broader views: "let me... reaffirm the inflexible resolve of Great Britain to aid the Indian people to fit themselves increasingly for the duties of self-government. Upon that course we have been embarked for many years, and we assign no limits to its ultimate fruition."

Churchill had two main doubts about India's ability to achieve a fully functioning and peaceful democracy at that time. First, he understood that India's ethnic- and religious-based caste system went against the basic democratic principle of equal rights. This was not a concern for India alone. Churchill had previously written that the real issue between the Boers and the British in the war almost thirty years before had been the refusal of the Dutch South Africans to "accept the equality of the Kafir." More broadly, Churchill embraced the American understanding of the necessity of equal rights for all if a true democracy is to be established. In an Independence Day speech in 1918, when America and Britain were allies in the First World War, he said of the Declaration of Independence, "[B]y it we lost an empire, and by it also we preserved an empire. By applying its principles and learning its lessons we have maintained our communion with the powerful Commonwealths our children have established beyond the seas." But India's or any other nation's acquisition of the "title deeds" of democracy required their embrace by the native population. Such an embrace by the Indians was doubtful in 1930.

At the time India was agitating for independence, the caste system was worse than Jim Crow segregation in the American South or apartheid in South Africa. Mahatma Gandhi and Jawaharlal Nehru, leaders of the Indian National Congress, which was agitating for independence, were both members of the upper castes. Gandhi was a member of the Vaishan, the merchant caste, and Nehru was a Brahmin, the highest caste of scholars and priests. Both opposed the abolition of the caste system, which consigned seventy-five million untouchables—the "pariahs"—to work in occupations such as garbage collection. The caste system enshrined the Caucasian Brahmins at the top but shunned, as if they were lepers, the mostly Negroid "pariahs" at the bottom. For Churchill, dominion status should not be granted to India until the caste system was abolished.

In Churchill's view, Nehru, a fellow old Harrovian, was more interested in seizing political power for himself than relieving the poverty of the unwashed millions in India. If Churchill had disdain for Nehru, he despised Gandhi. The Indian ascetic was a one-time

British barrister who had left the black robes of law for the white "diaper" he wore to dramatize his "saintly" role as mystic father of the Hindus. Churchill contemptuously described Gandhi as a "seditious Middle Temple lawyer, now posing as a fakir of a type well known in the East, striding half naked up the steps of the Vice Regal Palace to parley with the representative of the King."

Beyond the problem of the inequitable and undemocratic caste system, Churchill worried that the ethnic diversity of "India" would make democratic institutions impossible to maintain. The prospect of civil war was never far from his mind. In India there were over two hundred languages, as well as four dominant ethnic strains—Caucasoid, Mongoloid, Australoid, and Negroid. The relative success of the British administration of colonial India blinded many to the potential problems of this polyglot society set adrift. Churchill's father, Lord Randolph, had once said, "Our rule in India is, as it were, a sheet of oil spread out and keeping free from storms a vast and profound ocean of humanity."

It is too easy in the twenty-first century to condemn someone whose preconceptions and attitudes were the product of his Victorian upbringing. In 1930, the prevailing intellectual and literary voices of the time mocked the Victorian ideal of missionary do-good-ism and the sense of responsibility to take up "the white man's burden." They called for enfranchisement of the Indian masses.

If India became a dominion, Churchill charged, Hindus would drive out Muslims, and under Hindu civil service, profiteering and corruption would flourish. Nepotism, graft, and corruption would be "the hand maidens of a Brahmin domination." Above all, the Hindus would tyrannize "the untouchables," denying them all human rights.

About these "pariahs," Churchill said, "they were a multitude as big as a nation, men, women, and children deprived of hope and the status of humanity. Their plight is worse than slaves, because they have been taught to consent not only to a physical but psychic servitude and prostration."

Events in India bore out his warning. In March 1931, Muslim shopkeepers in Cawpore refused to close their stores during a period of mourning for a Hindu who had been executed for terrorism. In retaliation, Hindus attacked Muslim merchants in an orgy of murder, arson, and looting. Almost three hundred were killed.

Churchill, speaking at the Constitution Club on March 26, raised the specter of future mass murders and ethnic extermination:

> Wednesday's massacres at Cawpore, a name of evil import, are a portent. Because it is believed that we are about to leave the country, the struggle for power is now beginning between the Muslims and Hindus.

Churchill went on to say that these large-scale religious killings were only a foretaste of what loomed in the future:

> The bloody riot in which more than two hundred people lost their lives, with many other hundreds wounded, in which women and children were butchered in circumstances of bestial barbarity, their mutilated, violated bodies strewing the streets.... But the feud is only at its beginning.

As Churchill predicted, the violence went on unabated until, by the end of March, over a thousand were dead, the victims of Muslim and Hindu hatred.

On May 13, speaking in the House of Commons, Churchill blasted the Indian mill owners for calling for a boycott of British manufactured items. Brahmin and Hindu interests, he charged, were orchestrating the boycott, appealing to the people's superstition, prejudice, and greed. The effort would lead, he predicted, "to the spoliation of millions of people," and the Muslims would be persecuted, bled, and exploited.

The debate over dominion status for India resumed in the summer of 1931. Churchill said that the Labour government of the last two years, with the support of Conservatives, could claim four accomplishments—the boycott of British goods in India, the ruin of Lancashire manufacturing, the broken credit of India, and "the horrors of Cawpore." Muslims and Hindus were now "inflamed against each other."

Britain, however, was in the depths of the Great Depression, and the Indian issue was soon moved to the back burner. The Labour government fell, and a new National government was formed comprising all the parties. Ramsay MacDonald, a socialist, was again the prime minister and the public face of leadership, but the real power shifted to Stanley Baldwin, the Lord President of the Council. In the reassembling of cabinet posts, Churchill indirectly was offered a major post, but he refused, knowing the price of power would be his silence on the Indian issue.

There was a popular misconception that Churchill entered into his political exile in order to challenge the government's failure to see the menace of Hitler's Germany. It was not his refusal to appease Hitler that drove him from government but his earlier decision to not acquiesce to Baldwin and the Conservative Party on India.

Stanley Baldwin returned as prime minister for the second time in 1935, a decade after his first stint in the 1920s. Since the aftermath of World War I and the departure of Lloyd George, Baldwin had become the dominant political player in Britain. He was a superb politician. Churchill said of him, "He had his ear so close to the ground he had locusts in his ear."

In 1935, Baldwin—whose uncle, interestingly, was Rudyard Kipling, the novelist of Imperial India—again put forth an India Bill. It passed, despite Churchill's spirited opposition. Yet because the bill fell short of the radical demands of Gandhi and Nehru, the Indian National Congress rejected it.

It was not until 1947 that India achieved its independence, which had been repeatedly promised to its leaders during the war with Japan, which menaced India's borders. In 1947, Clement Attlee's Labour government achieved what Baldwin had failed to do. Churchill, by then, was the leader of the Conservative opposition, having been ousted from power in 1945. Churchill's friend and the king's cousin Lord Mountbatten had become the Viceroy of India in 1946. Mountbatten strongly supported Indian independence and persuaded Churchill not to mount a vigorous opposition. Churchill, who knew that, with Labour's large majority, independence was a *fait accompli*, grudgingly acceded, and Mountbatten went on to preside over the transition of power from the crown to Nehru, the new Indian prime minister.

Two-and-a-half million Indians would be slaughtered in 1947 because of the racial and religious hatred between Muslim and Hindu. One of the slain was Gandhi. The new Hindu government would do nothing, as Churchill feared, to rectify the evils of the caste system. Churchill's opposition to the dominion of India in the 1930s attested to his political conscience.

India has become a great nation and now has one of the strongest economies in the world. But even this happy progress, which Churchill would celebrate were he alive today, has not effaced his worry about the ethnic and religious fault lines of the subcontinent. India and Pakistan remain deeply hostile to one another, both equipped with nuclear weapons that could reignite on a new scale the violence Churchill hoped to prevent.

PART V

WORLD WAR II

CHAPTER 17

THE NAZI MENACE

CHURCHILL REPEATEDLY URGES BRITAIN TO TAKE HEED

I f there is one Churchillian prophesy that is indelibly etched in the minds of men, it is his continual warning about the rising threat of a rearming Germany. Churchill was the first to sound the alarm in 1932, and he continued to do so throughout the decade. The ensuing conflict, he would insist, was "an unnecessary war"; it could have been avoided if the Western democracies had sufficiently rearmed and stood up to Hitler diplomatically. Churchill was able to see the danger clearly because of two traits that were in short supply among the leaders of European democracies in the 1930s: a clearheaded assessment of the tyrannical and warlike character of the new German regime, and an appreciation of the solemn responsibility other nations had to maintain a margin of military superiority over the rising dictatorships.

There is a certain irony about Churchill's life: had his warnings been heeded and World War II averted, Churchill today might be a

117

forgotten figure. A further irony is that Hitler's political fortunes were inversely correlated with those of Churchill, who in the late 1920s had been expected to succeed Stanley Baldwin as the next Conservative prime minister. It was precisely because his far-sighted warnings were ignored or rejected that Britain turned to him in its gravest hour of need. And as we shall see, Churchill's prewar statesmanship became a model for the Western democracies in the Cold War, leading ultimately to a peaceful resolution of that conflict after a sustained effort spanning two generations.

Churchill's career in the 1930s is an excellent example of how he applied his insights to changing circumstances. His relentless criticism of appeasement, which in other times and in other contexts he thought reasonable, discredited the tactic for future statesmen. Yet he was not always a categorical opponent of appeasement, either before or after World War II. In 1950 he wrote to General Dwight Eisenhower about the difference: "Appeasement from weakness and fear is... fatal. Appeasement from strength is magnanimous, and might be the surest way to peace." In the 1930s, Britain and the other Western democracies had appeased from weakness. Churchill's aphoristic verdict on their policy: "An appeaser was one who would feed the crocodile hoping it would eat him last."

Critics of Churchill sometimes cite his differing views on appeasement as evidence of inconsistency or opportunism—the traits that are said to have led to his two changes of party. Churchill addressed this criticism, several years before the rise of Hitler, in his essay "Consistency in Politics," arguing, "The only way a man can remain consistent amid changing circumstances is to change with them while preserving the same dominating purpose." He added:

> It is inevitable that frequent changes should take place in the region of action. A policy is pursued up to a certain

point; it becomes evident at last that it can be carried no further. New facts arise which clearly render it obsolete; new difficulties, which make it impracticable. A new and possibly the opposite solution presents itself with over-whelming force.... It sometimes happens that the same men, the same Government, the same Party have to execute this *volte face*.

Churchill recognized the ominous character of the Nazi movement as early as 1930, more than two years before Hitler took power. In October of that year, the German ambassador to the United Kingdom, Prince Otto von Bismarck (a grandson of the Iron Chancellor) recorded that "Hitler had admittedly declared that he had no inten-tion of waging a war of aggression; he, Churchill, was convinced that Hitler or his followers would seize the first available opportunity to resort to armed force." As early as March 1931, Churchill predicted that the new "customs union" between Germany and Austria was a prelude to a future German annexation of Austria. If that happened, he added, Czechoslovakia would soon be menaced by Germans on three sides. The historian John Strawson observes:

The accuracy of Churchill's vision may be judged by a discourse Hitler made to his War Minister, the Command-ers-in-Chief of the three armed services, and his Foreign Ministry in November 1937, during which he expressed his determination to solve Germany's problem of *Leben-sraum* (living space). The precise date at which he would launch this operation would depend on circumstances, he said, but might be as early as 1938; the principal and most urgent objectives would be the overthrow of Austria and Czechoslovakia.[1]

Despite Churchill's early warning that England's "hour of weakness" would be "Europe's hour of danger," nothing could shake the British government from its enthusiasm for disarmament and appeasement. The same government in which Churchill had previously served was incapable of perceiving how changing circumstances were changing its duty; the government was incapable of executing a *volte face*.

So during the 1930s Churchill would regularly reel off from the back bench the increasing numbers of German weaponry and planes to an un-listening government. He sought to buttress his argument for increasing British preparedness, but his warnings went unheeded. Churchill would later call that period "his years in the wilderness," yet his exile from power and the clarity of his warnings provided him with the moral authority to lead the nation decisively when he finally became prime minister in May 1940. As he explained in the first volume of his memoirs of the Second World War, "My warnings over the last six years had been so numerous, so detailed, and were now so terribly vindicated, that no one could gainsay me."

The Churchill of those wilderness years has been likened to the Biblical prophet Jeremiah, who pleaded in the desert for the people of Israel to change their ways. Others compare him to Cassandra, the prophetess of Troy whom Apollo cursed with always being unheeded. The best comparison is that of the Athenian orator Demosthenes, who wielded his rhetorical gifts to warn of the military threat from Philip II of Macedon. The Athenians ignored Demosthenes' "philippics" until war was upon them.

Churchill's warnings about Hitler, however, were not simply about the numbers of tanks and planes. Armaments alone, he understood, were not the cause of war; it was the character and designs of a nation's leaders that determined war or peace. Churchill grasped early on that, contrary to conventional wisdom, the enthusiasm for disarmament after World War I would *increase* the likelihood of another European war, even without a Hitler. In the rush to disarmament, "conditions were swiftly created by the victorious Allies which, in the name of peace, cleared the way for the renewal of war.... The crimes of the vanquished find their background and their explanation, though not, of course, their pardon, in the follies of the victors. Without these follies crime would have found neither temptation nor opportunity."

Germany's stealthy rearmament in violation of the Versailles Treaty preceded the rise of Hitler by several years. Churchill was not in the least surprised that Germany sought to rearm, either legitimately through renegotiating the terms of Versailles, or in violation of the agreement: "It is natural that a proud people vanquished in war should strive to rearm themselves as soon as possible." But Churchill argued early and often that if France and England neglected to maintain military superiority over Germany, then general war would return to Europe. German rearmament began as early as 1921. Hitler was merely the spark that ignited pent-up German resentments in the aftermath of the awkward and unjust settlement of World War I. "Once Hitler's Germany had been allowed to rearm without active interference by the Allies and former associated Powers," Churchill wrote, "a second World War was almost certain."

Churchill's foreboding about Hitler preceded Hitler's arrival in the chancellor's office by several months, and his public warnings about the Nazi menace began remarkably early. On November 10, 1932, President Hindenburg of Germany asked Adolf Hitler, the leader of a plurality of deputies in the Reichstag who supported the Nazi line, to serve in his cabinet. Hitler answered that he would serve only as chancellor.

Four days later, Churchill rose from his seat in the back to comment on Germany's demand to rearm:

Do not delude yourselves. Do not let his Majesty's government believe—I am sure they do not believe—that all that
Germany is asking for is equal status.... That is not what
Germany is seeking. All these bands of Teutonic youths
marching through the streets and roads of Germany, with
the light of desire in their eyes, to suffer for their Father-
land, are not looking for their status. They are looking for
weapons, and when they have the weapons, believe me,
they will then ask for the return of lost territories and lost
colonies, and when that demand is made it cannot fail to
shake and possibly shatter to their foundations every one
of the countries I have mentioned [France, Poland, Belgium,
Romania, Czechoslovakia, and Yugoslavia].

The following month Churchill put the matter even more starkly in
another speech in the House: "The rise of Germany to anything like
military equality with France, or the rise of Germany or some other
ally or other to anything like military equality with France, Poland,
or the small states, means a renewal of a general European war."

Here again we see an example of Churchill's extraordinary perception and originality of thought. The Hungarian-born historian John
Lukacs argues that Churchill understood Hitler far better than Hitler
understood Churchill, and that this was to Churchill's great advantage
during the war.[2] (Hitler would later dismiss Churchill as "a superan-
nuated drunkard supported by Jewish gold.") How did Churchill
come to this early perception of the awful nature of the new German
regime? What gave him his unusual clarity of perception regarding
the character of Hitler and the likelihood of renewed European war
if the Western democracies did not stand up forcefully to Hitler? Once
again, Churchill's powerful historical imagination was the key.

By coincidence, Hitler's rise to power occurred as Churchill was
researching and writing the biography of his ancestor Sir John
Churchill, the first duke of Marlborough. His on-the-scene travels

included a visit to Blindheim ("Blenheim" in English), Bavaria, in the summer of 1932, shortly before Hitler became chancellor. It was while staying in Munich that Churchill nearly met Hitler. Over dinner with Ernst "Putzi" Hanfstaengl, a Harvard-educated acquaintance of his son, Randolph, Churchill was asked if he would like to meet Hitler. Churchill was staying at a hotel that Hitler visited almost daily; a dinner the following evening could easily be arranged. (Hanfstaengl was thought to have been acting on instructions from Hitler to inquire about such a meeting.) Churchill, after some reflection, said yes but then quizzed Hanfstaengl on Hitler's anti-Semitic views.

"Why is your chief so violent about the Jews? ... What is the sense of being against a man because of his birth? How can any man help the way he is born? Tell your boss anti-Semitism may be a good starter but it is a bad stayer." Churchill said he would put this question to Hitler if they met. When Hanfstaengl relayed Churchill's intentions, Hitler declined to proceed. "Thus," Churchill wrote with his usual immodesty, "Hitler lost his only chance of meeting me." The only other time the two figures came so near to one another was in 1916, when Major Churchill occupied a trench some sixty yards away from a dugout where Corporal Hitler was doing duty.

While in Germany in 1932, Churchill witnessed firsthand the Nazi marches on the roads near Blenheim. "I sensed the Hitler atmosphere," he wrote later in his memoirs of this trip. As he returned to Chartwell to dictate his biography of Marlborough, the duke's arch-foe, Louis XIV, was surely in his mind. Just as Hitler was more than simply a chancellor in a civil government, so too Louis XIV had been more than simply a king. "L'etat c'est moi" ("I am the state"), as he had put it himself.

Louis XIV took the cult of personality to ceremonial excess and nationalism to totalitarianism. The military might that he amassed in the name of French destiny spelled invasion and war for France's European neighbors. As he wrote the life of Marlborough, Churchill could see history repeating itself with the self-styled Führer filling the role of the Sun King. Much of Churchill's description of Louis XIV in *Marlborough* could apply to Hitler almost without amendment:

> During the course of his life Louis XIV was the curse and pest of Europe. No worse enemy of human freedom has ever appeared in the trappings of polite civilization. Insatiable appetite, cold, calculating ruthlessness, monumental conceit, presented themselves armed with fire and sword.... All was sacrificed to the worship of a single man.

So it was not difficult for Churchill to spot the modern German version of this absolute and rapacious ruler. Unlike many political leaders outside of Germany, Churchill read Hitler's memoir, *Mein Kampf*, and took it seriously. "When eventually he came to power," Churchill wrote, "there was no book which deserved more careful study from the rulers, political and military, of the Allied Powers. All was there...." Churchill described it as "the new Koran of faith and war: turgid, verbose, shapeless, but pregnant with its message." Most of Churchill's peers ignored or downplayed Hitler's writings. Journalists such as Vernon Bartlett said it was "unfair" to judge Hitler by his decade-old writings, and even David Lloyd George, Churchill's mentor and friend in the Liberal Party, insisted that Hitler wanted only friendship and peace with England. (Worse, Lloyd George wrote of Hitler to a friend, "I only wish we had a man of his supreme quality at the head of affairs in our country."[3]) It is remarkable how often Western leaders ignore the professed aims of radicals, whether Nazi, Communist, or Islamic. Churchill understood that it is best to take seriously what political figures say are their largest aims, rather than excuse their writings and speeches as "mere rhetoric." The world would have been spared much agony in recent centuries had more statesmen done so.

Churchill summarized Hitler's achievement in taking power in *The Gathering Storm*: "He had called from the depths of defeat the dark

and savage furies latent in the most numerous, most serviceable, ruth-
less, contradictory, and ill-starred race in Europe. He had conjured
up the fearful idol of an all-devouring Moloch of which he was the
priest and incarnation." Today we would call this "pattern recognition." For Churchill, foreseeing the successive steps of Hitler's aggression after the re-occupation of the Rhineland in 1936 was merely a
matter of logic, as simple as solving a basic algebra problem.

Churchill allowed that war was not inevitable. He wrote in 1935,
"We cannot tell whether Hitler will be the man who will once again
let loose upon the world another war in which civilization will irre-
trievably succumb, or whether he will go down in history as the man
who restored honor and peace of mind to the great Germanic
nation.... It is enough to say that both possibilities are open at the
present moment." Churchill added, however, that the hazard of war
meant that "we are forced to dwell upon the darker side of his work
and creed." Churchill's famous essay on Hitler, included in *Great
Contemporaries* (1937), while severely criticizing Hitler's anti-
Semitism and warlike inclinations, left open the possibility that
things might turn out all right.

Most of today's readers of that essay today do not realize that the
original version, published in *The Strand* magazine in 1935, was
much harsher. Churchill softened its tone for *Great Contemporaries*
under pressure from the Foreign Office, which feared offending Hitler. Sir Robert Vansittart, the permanent under-secretary, wrote to
Churchill that "it is hardly to be thought that this article would be at
all palatable to the powers that be in Germany.... [I]t might therefore
be questioned whether republication just now was advisable."
Churchill proceeded with his plans to include the essay, but deleted
a long passage deploring Hitler's violence against his domestic political enemies and ending with the question, "Can we really believe
that a hierarchy and society built upon such deeds can be trusted with
the possession of the most prodigious military machinery yet planned
among men?" Churchill succeeded in placating the diplomats, who

acknowledged that Churchill's changes "would certainly take a great deal of the sting out."

Knowing that weakness would tempt a vicious dictator like Hitler, Churchill was convinced that Britain's lassitude throughout the 1930s encouraged Hitler eventually to choose war. It was the inevitable nature of the regime Hitler had created. In a 1937 essay for *Colliers* magazine on the topic "Can America Keep Out of War?", Churchill described the inescapable logic of the situation:

> Thus we are confronted with a situation in Europe abhorrent to its peoples, including a great mass of German and Italian peoples, in which bands of competent, determined men under ruthless leadership find themselves alike unable to go or to stop. It may well be that the choice before Germany is a choice between an internal and an external explosion. But it is not Germany that will really choose. It is only that band of politicians who have obtained this enormous power, whose movements are guided by two or three men, who will decide the supreme issue of peace or war. To this horrible decision they cannot come unbiased. Economic and political ruin may stare them in the face, and the only means of escape may be victory in the field. They have the power to make war. They have the incentive to make war; nay, it may well be almost a compulsion.

Churchill's assessment seems straightforward in hindsight, but his warnings were widely dismissed at the time. Part of the rejection of Churchill's foresight was wishful thinking and fear. But part of it was a complete misapprehension of what Hitler represented, sometimes verging on approval of dictatorship as an acceptable or possibly preferable mode of government—a "wave of the future," like Communism. No one today wishes to recall that Hitler's National Socialism, like Marxist-Leninist Communism, had its own share of "useful idiots" willing to see in Nazism a benign progressive force. A prominent Anglican bishop claimed that Hitler "is a very religious man himself."[4] Another group of Anglican clergymen expressed their "boundless admiration for the moral and ethical side of the National Social program, its clear-cut stand for religion and Christianity." American intellectuals such as the historian Arnold Toynbee and the journalist Walter Lippmann also heaped praise on Hitler and his program in the mid-1930s.[5] Churchill was never fooled for a moment. He was always clear on the symbiotic nature of all modern totalitarian movements: "As Fascism sprang from Communism, so Nazism developed from Fascism. Thus were set on foot those kindred movements which were destined soon to plunge the world into even more hideous strife."

After the Reichstag passed the Enabling Act in 1933, severely restricting civil liberties, Churchill exercised his rhetorical skills in denouncing Hitler's Germany: "We watch with surprise and distress the tumultuous insurgence and ferocity and war spirit, the pitiless ill-treatment of minorities, the denial of normal protections of civilized society to large numbers of individuals solely on the grounds of race." The response in Germany was outrage. Berlin newspapers reported Hitler's "sharp warnings" about "Mr. Churchill's impudence." Hitler's admonition brought not silence but another speech.

To the Royal Society of St. George, Churchill said that the greatest danger lay not in Berlin but in "defeatist doctrines in Britain." "Nothing," said Churchill, "can save England if she will not save herself." Weaponry in defense, not words in diplomacy, should be the policy, said Churchill.

Churchill's predictions about the eventual achievement of German air superiority, stoutly denied or obfuscated by the government, likewise were less the product of clairvoyance than of concrete secret information relayed to him by a succession of informants inside the

British defense establishment and civil service. Churchill's chief source of information on the woeful inadequacy of British defenses was Major Desmond Morton. A neighbor of Churchill's in Kent, he had survived a bullet in the heart in World War I while serving in military intelligence. After the war he worked in the Foreign Office in intelligence and stayed in contact with some of the key civil servants.

In June 1933, Morton came over to Chartwell to report that Hitler had begun production of warplanes. The source of this information, Michael Creswell, informed Churchill that his boss, Foreign Secretary Sir John Simon, did not want to know "uncomfortable things."

Creswell was uneasy about handing over classified material for Morton to give to Churchill. He risked jail for violating the Official Secrets Act. Creswell shared Churchill's fear of the German build-up. He told Churchill that he admired him for speaking out in opposition to government policies but that he was apprehensive about handing documents to Churchill. Churchill answered, "Your first loyalty should be to your country, not the Foreign Office."

Ralph Wigram, Creswell's superior, was another civil servant gathering intelligence on German war production. A Wigram-to-Creswell-to-Morton-to-Churchill relay was set up.

When Churchill, on the floor of Parliament, named twenty-four German air force factories and called for the expansion of the Royal Air Force, Clement Atlee, the deputy leader of the governing coalition, called his words "nationalist and imperialist delusions" and denied that Hitler had aggressive conquest as an objective. But Germany achieved airpower parity with Britain by 1935.

Churchill needed no special insight to predict the *Anschluss* of Austria in 1937. Hitler had proclaimed this goal on the first page of *Mein Kampf*: "German Austria must return to the great German Motherland." Although Germany in 1936 disavowed any interest in absorbing Austria, Hitler was secretly fomenting unrest inside Austria and preparing plans for occupation. Mussolini's unfriendly attitude toward German expansion into Austria restrained Hitler's ambition temporarily, but the League of Nations' sanctions against Italy following Mussolini's aggression in Abyssinia had driven the Italians closer to Hitler, allowing him to proceed with his plan for the *Anschluss.*

Churchill wasted no time in predicting that Hitler would turn his attention to the southeast, starting with Czechoslovakia. "This mastery of Vienna," Churchill told the House on March 14, 1938, "gives to Nazi Germany military and economic control of the whole of the communications of Southeastern Europe...." Yet Britain was soon lulled back into a false sense of security.

His continual admonitions about the insufficiency of British defenses rattled Stanley Baldwin. In the House of Commons, sensing a flowering of dissent that threatened his prospects for the election of 1935, Baldwin made a promise to nip such dissent in the bud.

Addressing his king, the Parliament, and his country, Baldwin vowed, "His Majesty's government is determined, in no condition, to accept any inferiority with regard to what air force may be raised in Germany in the future." It was a promise he came to regret.

In March 1935, Churchill rose to contradict Baldwin's assertion of British superiority in the air. He informed Parliament that the Germans would have doubled their aircraft by 1936. "I am certain that Germany's preparations are infinitely more far reaching than our own." So, he continued, "they will be at least three and four times as strong as we."

Despite his attacks on Baldwin from the back bench, Churchill took the stump for Conservative candidates in marginal districts. By doing so, he hoped to persuade the prime minister to include him in his cabinet in some military or defense role.

The pipe-smoking Baldwin, the very image of stolid old John Bull, radiated comforting assurance to British voters. To the left, he pledged no new armaments and to the right no new taxes. The Conservatives won a massive victory on November 14, 1935.

Churchill waited for a cabinet appointment that never came. The new chancellor of the exchequer, Neville Chamberlain, told Baldwin that Churchill would be a voice in the cabinet for rearmament. Baldwin agreed that Churchill's "preparedness" would mean more money for defense. That spelled deficits in a time of a depressed economy.

In March, Churchill rose to challenge the government's newly released defense white paper, which promised only a scant increase in the number of RAF fighter planes to defend against an enlarged Luft-waffe: "Virtuous motives, trammeled by inertia and timidity, are no match for armed and resolute weakness. A sincere love of peace is no excuse for muddling hundreds of millions of humble folk into total war." He closed portentously: "Doom marches on." And indeed Hitler marched his troops westward into the Rhineland on March 7, 1936. Churchill now warned that if the Nazi coup were to pass unchallenged, Austria would be Hitler's next objective, and "if Austria perishes, Czechoslovakia becomes indefensible."

Churchill had long pressed for a new Ministry of Defense that would consolidate preparedness efforts. The press now echoed that call. Churchill was the obvious candidate, but Chamberlain argued against him, saying that the appointment of Churchill would only inflame Hitler.

The Nazi reptile, as Churchill predicted, now swallowed Austria. Her chancellor, Kurt Schuschnigg, capitulated to Hitler's demands in February 1938. When Hitler lauded his "understanding" and his warm-hearted willingness to bring Austria and Germany closer, Churchill snorted, "When a boa constrictor wants to eat his victims, he first covers him with saliva."

Churchill had predicted that Czechoslovakia, Austria's eastern neighbor, would be Hitler's next prey. Neville Chamberlain, who in May 1937 had moved from 11 Downing Street to Number 10, was as committed to the policy of appeasement as Baldwin had been. Chamberlain said that the situation in Europe was "relaxed," and there was no need for alarm. Churchill saw it differently, "After a boa constrictor has devoured its prey, it often has a considerable digestive spell."

In the House of Commons, Churchill rose to express his alarm:

> For five years I have talked to the House on these mat-
> ters—not with very great success. I have watched this
> famous island descending incontinently, fecklessly the stair-
> way which leads to a dark gulf. It is a fine broad stairway
> at the beginning but after a bit the carpet ends. A little
> farther on there are only flagstones and a little farther on
> still these break beneath your feet....

In the summer of 1938, Hitler and his henchmen were inciting unrest among ethnic Germans in the Sudetenland, the western region of Czechoslovakia. The voice of the establishment, the *Times*, suggested a plebiscite to allow the Germans of the Sudetenland to choose whether to join the Reich.

Chamberlain had confided to his parliamentary secretary how he would run foreign policy when he became prime minister. Convinced that he could talk to Hitler man-to-man and bring about a settlement of the crisis, he visited the Führer in his mountain lair at Berchtes-gaden. After a twenty-minute tirade about the Germans in the Sude-tenland, Hitler asked if Britain would support their right of self-determination. Chamberlain agreed and sold the deal to the French. An alarmed Churchill denounced the plan to balkanize Czechoslovakia in the face of Nazi threats.

Hitler reneged on the self-determination proposal. Brandishing a map marking the area that must be occupied by German troops, he said the Sudeten problem had to be solved by October 1. The threat was reinforced by a German mobilization along the Oder River, its border with Czechoslovakia.

Chamberlain again flew to see Hitler, where he accepted the new terms and agreed to advise the Czechs to do likewise. Jan Masaryk of Czechoslovakia, however, was defiant: "The nation of St. Wenceslas, John Hus, and Thomas Masaryk [his father] will not be slaves."

The Munich Conference followed. Masaryk, faced with the desertion of his British and French allies, had to acquiesce. Chamberlain and the French premier, Édouard Daladier, signed the agreement, along with Hitler and his Axis partner Mussolini.

In London, Churchill said of the British submission, "It was sordid, squalid, sub-human, and suicidal. The sequel to the sacrifice of London would be the sacrifice of lives, our peoples' lives."

Later, Churchill would tell friends that Chamberlain had faced a choice of war or dishonor. "He chose dishonor and he will get war anyway."

Yet, to the British people, Chamberlain had chosen peace and rescued the nation from the precipice of war. As Chamberlain told the cheering millions in Britain, alluding to Disraeli's triumphant return from the Berlin Conference in 1878, "My good friends, this is the second time in our history that there has come back from Germany to Downing Street peace with honour. I believe it is peace for our time."

To those in Parliament who had rejoiced at the settlement, Churchill delivered a biblical condemnation of it:

> They should know that we have passed an awful milestone in our history, when the whole equilibrium of Europe has been deranged, and that the terrible words have for the time being been pronounced against the Western democracies, "Thou art weighed in the balance and found wanting." And do not suppose that this is the end.

He closed ominously:

> This is the beginning of the reckoning. This is the first sip,
> the first foretaste of the bitter cup which will be proffered
> to us year by year, unless by a supreme recovery of moral
> health and martial vigour, we rise again and take our stand
> for freedom as in the olden time.

The motto on Churchill's coat of arms bespoke his fortunes in the 1930s: *Fiel pero desdichado,* "Faithful but unfortunate." As the beginning of the decade's last year opened, Churchill's prophecies had been true and resolute, but, unfortunately, his country had not heeded him.

The lessons most people take from the spectacle of Churchill's unheeded warnings of the 1930s are the folly of appeasement and the danger of military unpreparedness. Both lessons are valid, but at the core of Churchill's prophetic insight was an appreciation of how human nature—especially an evil human nature—plays out in politics and how the patterns of history cannot be willfully swept aside by wishful thinking.

CHAPTER 18

THE NAZI-SOVIET PACT STUNS THE WORLD

CHURCHILL IS NOT SURPRISED

O f all the surprises in the run-up to the outbreak of World War II, few events shocked the world as much as the Molotov-Ribbentrop Pact of August 1939, in which Germany and the Soviet Union committed to non-aggression against each other, and which paved the way for partitioning Poland by force of arms. The idea of collaboration between Nazis and Communists was unthinkable. The historic enmity between Germany and Russia was supercharged under Hitler and Stalin. Hitler's seething hatred of Communism was well known, and the Soviet Union's resentment toward Germany from World War I was equally obvious.

One of the few who was not surprised was Winston Churchill. He observed later that "This violent and unnatural reversal of Russian policy was a transmogrification of which only totalitarian states are capable... only totalitarian despotism could have faced the odium of such an unnatural act."

As early as 1919, Churchill, then a cabinet minister in Lloyd George's government, foresaw the potential for German-Soviet collaboration. He argued, "Our policy must be directed to prevent a union between German militarism and Russian Bolshevism, for if that occurred, those tyrants would swiftly crush the little states which lie between them." In 1939, the non-aggression pact between the Nazis of Germany and the Communists made geopolitical if not ideological sense to Churchill. It set the table for the carve-up and conquest of Poland, which lay between them.

The contrast between Churchill's clarity of foresight in this instance and the willful disregard of his warnings by his peers is yet another case study in the disastrous effects of appeasement and self-delusion about the character of tyrannical regimes and wishful thinking about the future course of events.

The intellectual community of writers and journalists that does so much to shape public opinion was flabbergasted by the announcement. Just a few years before, in the Spanish Civil War, the Nazis had sided with the Nationalists led by General Franco while the Soviets backed the pro-Communist Loyalists. In America as well as in Britain, many Communist sympathizers ceased their support of the Soviet Union. During the Great Depression of the 1930s, many "fellow travelers" had enlisted in the Communist cause to fight the fascism of Hitler, Mussolini, and Franco. Now Communist Russia had shaken hands with the devil. But many hardcore Communists, like the playwright Lillian Hellman and other Hollywood writers, proved their party credentials by toeing the Kremlin line and abruptly halting their attacks on Hitler and Nazism.

While most looked at Nazism and Communism through an ideological lens, Churchill's vision suffered no such distortion. He compared not the contrasting ideals of the two dominant "isms" of the twentieth century but rather the results. The professed objectives of a "master race" and a "dictatorship of the proletariat" may have appeared to be opposites, but the totalitarian means by which each regime pursued its goals were of the same character. Churchill was always clear about the symbiotic nature of all modern totalitarian movements, as he explained in his World War II memoirs: "As Fascism sprang from Communism, so Nazism developed from Fascism. Thus were set on foot those kindred movements which were destined soon to plunge the world into even more hideous strife." Churchill's son, Randolph, told me that his father once remarked, "Polar opposites—no, polar the same!" Churchill despised both. "I will not pretend if I had to choose between Communism and Nazism, I would choose Communism. I hope not to be called on to survive in either."

Yet the world continued to look at Communism and Fascism as if they were opposites. Left is left and right is right, and never the twain shall meet—certainly not the far left and far right. But Churchill saw Communism and Fascism not as occupying opposite ends of a straight line but rather as abutting each other at the top of a circle, much as 365 degrees is close to 5 degrees.

Churchill also viewed the rival powers of Russia and Germany in a historical, as well as geopolitical, context. It was the German government, after all, that transported Lenin back to St. Petersburg to foment revolution. Under the Czarist and Soviet regimes, Russian foreign policy remained constant. Both cast a covetous eye upon Poland and toward control of the other Slavic peoples to their west.

For Churchill the geopolitical strategist, Hitler's *Anschluss* of March 1938 ought to have compelled Britain immediately to seek some accommodation with the Soviet Union. Not doing so would force Stalin to make a deal with Hitler. In the spring and summer of

1938, Churchill repeated his warning of 1919 that "German militarism" would join up with "Bolshevism."

As early as 1934, Churchill, who once described Communism as
"a ghoul descending from a pile of skulls," was mulling over the possibility of making some arrangement with Russia to confront the
aggressive designs of the power-hungry, land-greedy Hitler. While
assessing the figures of rising German air strength in the House,
Churchill urged "the full inclusion" of Soviet Russia in the emerging
defensive bloc of which Britain, France, and Poland were already a
part.

Then two years later, Churchill began lunching with Russia's
ambassador, Ivan Maisky. The Soviet envoy had sent Churchill a copy
of a speech that he had recently given about Russia's desire to be a
partner in the effort to curb Hitler. Baldwin and the Conservative
Party did not share Churchill's views. From the time Churchill began
urging an accommodation with the Soviet Union, his own ruling
party's leadership stood resolutely in the way. In the campaign of
1935, Baldwin made peace part of his platform. The Conservative
leader pledged, "I am not going to get this country into war with
anybody, for the League of Nations or anybody else or for anything
else.... [S]upposing the Russians and Germans got fighting and the
French went in as the allies of Russia—owing to the appalling pact
they made, you would not feel you were obliged to go to help France,
would you?"

Baldwin closed his boilerplate stump speech in the 1935 campaign
saying, "If there is any fighting in Europe, I should like to see the
Bolshies and Nazis doing it." It triggered great applause at every stop.
Baldwin, who never needed to consult polling data, had a thorough
understanding of British sentiment. If such a conflict ever occurred,
Baldwin wanted to see Hitler come out on top. So he replaced the
pro-French Sir Eric Phipps as the British ambassador to Germany with

Sir Neville Henderson, whom career Foreign Office men, muttering under their breath, called the "Nazi Ambassador to Berlin."

As Hitler's belligerence mounted, Baldwin and then his successor, Chamberlain, assured their fellow appeasers that Hitler would fight the Russians and leave the British alone. Yet to allay their anxiety about Hitler's antics in the Reichstag, they were ready to go to the negotiating table and find out what the Führer wanted. They were convinced Hitler had his price. On the other hand, the Conservative government treated any suggestion that British diplomats might talk to their Soviet counterparts as absurd.

When Neville Chamberlain became prime minister in 1937, this one-sided diplomacy was reinforced. He chose as his top civil servant advisor Sir Horace Wilson, a Hitler sympathizer and a Francophobe, who regarded any talk of treaties with the Soviets as tantamount to treason. As the gatekeeper to the prime minister, Wilson squelched Churchill's recommendations to approach the Soviets. Wilson's bias towards Germany merely reflected the British establishment. As much as the British ruling class sneered at the crude Hitler, they feared Bolshevism more.

Prevailing opinion began to change when Hitler used his base in the Sudetenland to crush the rest of Czechoslovakia in March 1939. The Munich agreement, which Chamberlain had signed the previous fall and had been regarded as deliverance from war, was now seen as a disgrace. The press, except for the *Times*, was now urging Chamberlain to put the vindicated Churchill back into the Cabinet.

Churchill had predicted this falling of dominoes, one by one: the occupation of the Rhineland, the *Anchluss* in Austria, and then the takeover of Czechoslovakia. Each extension of Nazi rule added to the proof of the Churchillian doctrine that appeasement leads not to peace but to further conquest and war. Poland, Churchill now prophesied, would be Hitler's next objective. Churchill once again urged a military pact among Britain, France, and Russia. With the destruction of Czechoslovakia, Britain and France needed an eastern European country that was more powerful than Poland. They had to have as an ally a nation strong enough to withstand the German Wehrmacht, thus forcing Hitler to wage a two-front war. That could only be Russia. Churchill said in the House, "The wisest course is to forget the Bolshevik past and forge Britain, France, and Russia in a 'Triple Alliance.'"

But Churchill's advice was rejected again. If any defense arrangements had to be made to prevent war, Chamberlain and his foreign secretary preferred a London-Berlin-Rome alliance, not one with Moscow.

The tragedy of this shortsightedness arises from the real prospect that the Soviet Union might have embraced an entente with Britain and France if a good faith offer had been made. Maisky listened approvingly to Churchill in the Strangers (Visitors) Gallery in the House of Commons. Maisky then launched a series of dinners at his embassy for those members of Parliament and the press who rejected the arguments of appeasement. Max Litinov, the Soviet foreign secretary, was thinking along the same lines as Maisky. Litinov, like Maisky, was a Soviet Jew and an Anglophile. Both of them had spent years in London.

On March 18, 1939, Litinov proposed an immediate conference in Bucharest. Those to be invited were Russia, Romania, Poland, Britain, France, and Turkey. Together they would form a defensive front against the threatening Reich. This Soviet overture was curtly rejected by Chamberlain and Halifax.

On April 10, Churchill again pleaded for enlistment of the Soviets into the anti-Nazi cause:

> The other day I tried to show the House the great interest
> that Russia has against a further Eastward expansion of

Nazi power.... I am sure we shall hear from the Government the steps they are taking to receive the fullest cooperation of Russia.

But privately Churchill was not so sure. He knew the prejudices of Chamberlain and Halifax. Yet, this time they did respond, if grudgingly. They asked Russia to affirm the independence of Poland but then offered no assistance in the defense of Poland.

In the Kremlin, Litinov was now desperate. Patience, however, was not a virtue of the paranoid Stalin. He had little love for the Western democracies, which had showed no respect to him and the Soviet Union for the last decade. Litinov then proposed in a document that was sent to Paris and London a recommendation for a three-power, anti-Nazi conference to take place in May.

Sir Horace Wilson, Chamberlain's *éminence grise*, was aghast. What if Hitler discovered the document? Would he blame Britain for it? It was the last chance for a British, French, and Soviet alliance, and Chamberlain threw it away.

After two weeks of British silence, Stalin dismissed Litinov and replaced him with Vyacheslav Molotov. Of Molotov Churchill wrote, "I have never seen a human being who more perfectly represented the modern conception of a robot." The mechanical, emotionless Molotov admired German efficiency and ruthlessness. With Molotov, Stalin would begin his dealings with the Nazis. Simultaneously, Molotov recalled Maisky, Litinov's pro-English diplomatic partner. Stalin, who never hid his anti-Semitism, told the party congress, in effect, that Molotov, who is no Jew, speaks directly for him.

Churchill, exasperated by the change of climate in the Kremlin, told the House in May:

If His Majesty's government now reject and cast away the indispensable aid of Russia and so lead us in the worst of

all ways, into the worst of all wars, they will have ill-
deserved the confidence and, I will add, the generosity with
which they have been treated by their fellow countrymen.

Chamberlain's answer to the declining confidence by his own party
was to vow support for Poland's independence. Halifax, representing
the British government, was now talking with the Poles, but he was
also meeting with the Germans, with whom he was siding in their bid
to take back the Polish port of Danzig.

British relations with Molotov were now one-sided. Discussions
of military mutuality were met by Molotov's stone face. He was talking only with Joachim von Ribbentrop, his German counterpart. In
August, Hitler sent Ribbentrop to Moscow to conclude a non-aggression pact. It was agreed that Russia would sit by as Hitler moved into
Poland but that he would stop there.

As August drew to a close, Nazi troops gathered on the Polish
border. War came in the early hours of Sunday, September 1, when
German Panzer divisions rumbled across the Polish frontier. A sad-
dened Chamberlain told his countrymen that Britain was now at war.
He then called back Churchill to be First Lord of the Admiralty, for
the second time.

On October 1, Churchill, on the BBC, delivered his famous epi-
grammatic assessment of the Soviet-Nazi non-aggression pact:

> I cannot forecast the action of Russia. It is a riddle, wrapped
> in a mystery inside an enigma; but perhaps there is a key.
> That key is Russian national interest.

He went on to suggest that German dreams for eastern European
domination would eventually intrude into the Soviet sphere.

By the following May, Churchill was prime minister in a coalition
government. In the summer of the following year, 1941, Hitler invaded

Russia. Churchill had long predicted that after Western Europe was subjugated, Hitler would turn against his fellow signatory to the infamous non-aggression pact. From the outset, Churchill had been convinced that the deal between the two dictators to carve up Poland would collapse under the weight of its own corruption. Not only had he expected the attack to occur some time in the spring months, but he had instructed his envoys to communicate that intelligence to a disbelieving Stalin.

As Hitler's orders were brutally executed by his high command, Churchill strolled the lawns at Chequers, the prime minister's country residence, to ponder the new geopolitical configuration. His parliamentary secretary, John (Jock) Colville, wondered how the prime minister, with his implacable hatred of Communism, could team up with the Soviet dictator. Churchill replied, "If Hitler invaded the realms of Hell, I would at least make a favorable reference to the Devil in the House of Commons."

Churchill was the first to prophesy the possibility of German militarism's allying itself with Russian Bolshevism, and he was the first to predict the short shelf life of such an alliance. Again we see how Churchill's predictive abilities did not require any supernatural powers of clairvoyance. It was sufficient for him to perceive the character of tyrannical, aggressive regimes and to keep in mind the lessons of history. Ultimately, as Churchill himself explained it, understanding this episode was a matter of moral clarity:

> It is a question whether Hitler or Stalin loathed it most. Both were aware that it could only be a temporary expedient. The antagonisms between the two empires and systems were mortal.... A moral may be drawn from this, which is of homely simplicity—"Honesty is the best policy."... Crafty men and statesmen will be shown misled by all their elaborate calculations. But this is the signal

instance.... If a Government has no moral scruples, it often seems to gain great advantages and liberties of action, but "All comes out even at the end of the day, and all will come out yet more even when all the days are ended."

CHAPTER 19

CHURCHILL IS CERTAIN OF VICTORY

DESPITE BLEAK CIRCUMSTANCES, HE PROFESSES FAITH IN THE OUTCOME AS EARLY AS 1942

In hindsight, the Allied victory over Nazi Germany seems to have been a foregone conclusion. Germany had made the fatal mistake, once again, of fighting a two-front war. Churchill's soaring oratory, promising from the outset victory against all odds, reassured successive generations that right would triumph over might. And once the United States joined the war, with its enormous industrial might and manpower, the outcome was settled.

Despite Churchill's oratory and obvious personal determination, it was never a foregone conclusion that Britain would survive the Nazi onslaught, even with U.S. assistance. The victory Churchill proclaimed appeared a chimera; Britain would be incapable for several years ahead of establishing a presence again on the European continent. It was not even assured that Churchill would survive as prime minister beyond his first few weeks in office. His own Conservative Party was unenthusiastic about his premiership; but for Labour support in a coalition government, Churchill would not have become prime minister in the first place. "This is not the last war administration by a long way," one leading member of Churchill's party said. His Downing Street private secretary, John Colville, wrote that "Seldom can a Prime Minister have taken office with the Establishment... so dubious of the choice and so prepared to find its doubts justified." Nearly forgotten today is that Churchill had to face down two no-confidence motions in the House of Commons in the early years of the war, as criticism mounted against him of setbacks and military mistakes.

Privately, Churchill had his own doubts too. Although he expressed perfect confidence in his memoirs, the night he became prime minister—May 10, 1940—he told an aide: "I hope that it is not too late. I am very much afraid that it is. We can only do our best." His oration that included the famous lines, "We shall fight on the beaches, we shall fight on the landing ground, we shall fight in the fields and in the streets, we shall fight in the hills. *We shall never surrender*," has a revealing coda. During the prolonged applause that erupted in the House of Commons when Churchill delivered this climactic line, Churchill turned to a Member sitting close by and remarked *sotto voce*, "If they do land, we'll beat the bastards over the head with the butt-ends of broken beer bottles, which is bloody all we've got."

Even with the entry of the United States after the Japanese bombing of Pearl Harbor on December 7, 1941, there were reasons to doubt that the Allies could force Germany to accept unconditional surrender. Although Britain turned back Germany's air assault in the Battle of Britain and scored some battlefield success on the periphery of the war, its position throughout the first half of 1941 remained desperate. It was still fighting alone, with Germany's submarine campaign choking off badly needed supplies from overseas. Not until Hitler invaded the Soviet Union in June 1941 did Britain see its prospects improve, though a quick Soviet defeat at the hands of Hitler, which appeared likely in the early months of the German offensive, threatened to increase Britain's peril. Churchill told the House of Commons that a German attack on the Soviet Union would be "no more than a prelude to an attempted invasion of the British Isles."

As we have seen, Churchill anticipated that Hitler would betray the Molotov-Ribbentrop Pact, and Churchill tried to warn Stalin directly of the growing peril in April 1941, two months before Hitler launched his attack. Stalin sent no reply. In his World War II memoirs, Churchill was savagely critical of Stalin's shortsightedness: "War is mainly a catalogue of blunders, but it may be doubted whether any mistake in history has equaled that of which Stalin and the Communist chiefs were guilty when they cast away all possibilities in the Balkans and supinely awaited, or were incapable of realizing, the fearful onslaught which impended from Russia.... We have hitherto rated them as selfish calculators. In this period they were proved simpletons as well."

A week before the attack, Churchill sent a cable to President Roosevelt predicting that a German attack on the Soviet Union "was imminent." After the attack began, Churchill wasted no time in aligning Britain with the Soviet Union against Hitler, despite Churchill's long-standing opposition to Soviet Communism:

> The Nazi regime is indistinguishable from the worst features of Communism. It is devoid of all theme and principle except appetite and racial domination. It excels all forms of human wickedness in the efficiency of its cruelty and ferocious aggression. No one has been a more consistent opponent of Communism than I have been for the last twenty-five years. I will unsay no word that I have spoken about it. But all this fades away before the spectacle that

is now unfolding. The past, with its crimes, its follies, and
its tragedies, flashes away.

The United States' entry into World War II is regarded as the turning
point, but FDR's remark to Churchill over the telephone on the evening of December 7, 1941, "We're all in the same boat now," was not
necessarily true. Only Hitler's gratuitous declaration of war against
the United States a few days later assured the total American commitment to the European theater of the war. There was considerable
sentiment in the U.S. to make war on Japan alone and to stay out of
the European conflict. Hitler's improvident lunge against the U.S.,
made in a typical fit of overconfidence, solved that political problem
for FDR.

At this point it is useful to recall the position of the Allies. The last
days of 1941 were hardly a time for optimism for the two English-
speaking allies. As the year 1942 opened, Hitler could be reasonably
confident of victory. The swastika flew over all of Europe, whose
conquered nations were now virtually German provinces. The core
of the American Pacific Fleet was shattered at Pearl Harbor. Its naval
bases in Guam and Wake Island were the ports from which the U.S.
Navy once policed the Pacific in the so-called "American lake." Now
those naval stations were overrun by the Japanese. The feeble air
power of the United States could not defend either of its coasts, and
its armies, undermanned and under-equipped, were unready.

After the fall of France and the Blitz that turned much of London
into ashes and rubble, Britain was barely hanging on. The losses in
their Pacific fleet far exceeded those of the United States. The Rising
Sun flag now flew over Hong Kong and Singapore. Burma, the gateway to India, had been invaded. Additionally, Field Marshal Rommel's
Afrika Korps was routing the British army in Libya and Tunisia.

Yet this was the moment at which Churchill became confident of
ultimate victory. Though he wrote that "I could not foretell the course

of events," he was certain of the outcome: "So we had won the war after all! England would live.... How long the war would last or in what fashion it would end, no man could tell, nor did I at this moment care.... Hitler's fate was sealed. Mussolini's fate was sealed. As for the Japanese, they would be ground to powder." On that fateful evening, Churchill added, "I went to bed and slept the sleep of the saved and thankful."

Churchill's chapter about Pearl Harbor in the third volume of his World War II memoirs, *The Grand Alliance*, contains one of his most memorable passages about America:

> Silly people—and there are many, not only in enemy countries—might discount the force of the United States. Some said they were soft, others that they would never be united. They would fool around at a distance. They would never come to grips. They would never stand the blood-letting. Their democracy and system of recurrent elections would paralyze their war effort. They would be just a vague blur on the horizon to friend or foe. Now we should see the weakness of this numerous but remote, wealthy, and talkative people. But I had studied the American Civil War, fought out to the last desperate inch. American blood flowed in my veins. I thought of a remark which Edward Grey had made to me more than thirty years before—that the United States is like "a gigantic boiler. Once the fire is ignited under it there is no limit to the power it can generate."

This now unswerving conviction of eventual victory was echoed in Churchill's closing words to the U.S. Congress three weeks later:

> It is not given to us to peer into the mysteries of the future. Still, I avow my hope and faith, sure and inviolate, that in

the days to come the British and American peoples will, for
their own safety and for the good of all, walk together side
by side in majesty, in justice, and in peace.

In his words to the U.S. Congress, Churchill was eloquently restating
a conviction he first felt with the president's call after Pearl Harbor:
an Allied victory was now only a matter of time. It would require
another three and a half years of hard fighting, but Churchill's confidence was vindicated.

CHAPTER 20

A RARE MISS

CHURCHILL MISPERCEIVES THE CHANCES OF D-DAY SUCCESS

The D-Day landing of June 6, 1944, ranks as the boldest and most successful large-scale invasion in military history. It would seem on the surface like the kind of audacious stroke that Churchill would fully support. Yet his usual prescience failed him in this case. Although he supported an invasion of Europe in principle, Churchill was lukewarm at best in his support for Operation Overlord, as the D-Day invasion plan was code named. Worried up to the last minute that it might be a disastrous failure, Churchill urged alternative invasion plans, to the exasperation of his American allies. A month before D-Day, when details of the invasion plan were nearly complete, Churchill thought that the Allies would be fortunate to command the French beachhead by Christmas.

Churchill knew when he became prime minister in 1940 that a second front against Germany on the European mainland would, in the fullness of time, be necessary to defeat Hitler, but there were three reasons for Churchill's deep misgivings about D-Day. First, in this rare instance his historical perspective misled him. He feared a repetition of the costly World War I stalemate of the trenches, despite the changes in mechanized warfare since then. Second, his own military's performance in the war had undermined his confidence in them. And third, for a variety of strategic and political reasons, Churchill favored an invasion elsewhere—through what he called the "soft underbelly" of southeastern Europe, or through the Arctic approaches to northern Europe. He favored anywhere but Atlantic France.

Practically from the first hours after the German invasion of Russia in June 1941, when Churchill had rushed to embrace Stalin as an ally against Hitler, the Soviet Union pressured Britain (and the United States) to open a second front on the continent as soon as possible—a prospect that was totally unrealistic in 1941. "The British Communists," Churchill wrote bitterly after the war, "who had hitherto done their worst... and had denounced 'the capitalist and imperialist war,' turned about again overnight and began to scrawl the slogan 'Second Front Now,' upon the walls and hoardings." In Stalin's first personal message to Churchill, a few weeks after the German invasion, he urged Britain to open a second front in Europe at "this most propitious moment." "The Russians never understood to the smallest degree," Churchill wrote, "the nature of the amphibious operation necessary to disembark and maintain a great army upon a well-defended hostile coast. Even the Americans were at this time largely unaware of the difficulties.... It could not be ready even on a minor scale before the summer of 1943." Indeed, Churchill talked Roosevelt out of an earlier invasion—Operation Sledgehammer—in 1942, and persuaded him to back Torch, the offensive in North Africa, instead.

Then Churchill successfully opposed the American successor plan for an invasion in France in 1943—Operation Roundup.

American commanders, including George Marshall, Dwight Eisenhower, and even Douglas MacArthur out in the Pacific, were initially dismayed by the proposal for Torch, but they quickly came to appreciate Churchill's logic. His argument was that with control of the Mediterranean, North Africa would become the gateway to Europe, resulting in the subsequent engagement of the Allies with German troops. A North African campaign would compel the Nazis to redirect troops away from their campaign against the Soviet Union and relieve some pressure on the Soviets as much as a second front in Europe would do. Churchill was correct: Germany's victory over American forces in the battle of Kasserine Pass in Tunisia in 1942 was achieved in part by troops sent from the Russian front to back up General Erwin Rommel. And a successful North African campaign could be launched soon, while an invasion of France could not be carried out for at least a year or more.

Churchill eventually traveled to Moscow in 1942 to personally deliver to Stalin the hard news that there would be no second front that year. Stalin, not pleased, responded with rage. An early second front, Churchill informed Stalin, was simply not yet possible. For the time being, Churchill said, the Allies would have to concentrate on attacks on the periphery, starting in North Africa and then proceeding against Italy.

In the background was Churchill's vivid memory of the appalling and unproductive trench warfare of World War I. Contemplating an invasion of the continent through the Atlantic approaches to France, Churchill wrote:

> I was not convinced that this was the only way of winning the war, and I knew that it would be a very heavy and

hazardous adventure. The fearful price we had had to pay
in human life and blood for the great offensives of the First
World War was graven in my mind. Memories of the
Somme and Passchendaele and many lesser frontal attacks
were not to be blotted out by time or reflection. It still
seemed to me, after a quarter of a century, that fortifica-
tions of concrete and steel armed with modern fire-power,
and fully manned by trained, resolute men, could only be
overcome by surprise in time or place by turning their
flanks, or by some new mechanical device like the tank.
Superiority of bombardment, terrific is it may be, was no
final answer.

After the United States entered the war following Pearl Harbor,
Churchill seems to have lent his support to an American proposal for
an invasion through France chiefly because he feared that without an
aggressive European strategy, American leaders might decide to concentrate their main war effort against Japan instead of Germany, as
indeed many Americans desired. This was not a passing worry. Shifting the main American focus from Europe to Japan was still a prospect
as late as 1943 and was constantly on Churchill's mind. But in all of
the planning councils, Churchill and his staff laid roadblocks in the
way of the invasion plans. In the 1943 Quebec conference with FDR,
where Overlord was the chief topic of discussion, Churchill pressed
for a rule whereby the invasion would be called off if there were more
than twelve mobile German divisions in northern France available to
respond to the attack.

In his frequent conversations with General Eisenhower, Churchill
continually repeated his misgivings about a cross-Channel invasion.
Eisenhower recalled that Churchill talked about William the Con-
queror's successful cross-Channel invasion in 1066, along with details

of Julius Caesar's invasion before the time of Christ. From writing his *History of the English-Speaking Peoples*, which he suspended in 1939 when halfway done, Churchill knew a great deal about the tides, the vagaries of weather, and the logistics of sea transport on the choppy Channel. Churchill also enumerated the Spanish Armada's heavy losses in troops and ships in its attempted invasion in 1588. "Ike," he explained, "they were the Nazi juggernaut of that day."

Churchill's second reason for doubt was more agonizing for him: he lacked confidence in his own military commanders. From the outset of the war, Churchill had the same problem that faced Abraham Lincoln in the Civil War—finding battlefield commanders competent and eager to fight effectively. Despite some battlefield successes in North Africa and the Middle East, Churchill was consistently disappointed with most of his military commanders. He made frequent changes in command and quarreled endlessly with his service chiefs.

One disastrous action in particular deepened Churchill's doubts about the capacity of his commanders to carry out a European invasion. In August 1942, a force of about six thousand mostly Canadian troops launched a raid on the French coastal city of Dieppe. The raid lasted only about nine hours, during which time about a thousand of the attacking troops were killed and two thousand taken prisoner. Two British planes were shot down for every downed German plane. The incident was a debacle in the eyes of all except the commanders who organized and directed it; they declared victory in their after-action reports to the prime minister. According to the historian Max Hastings, the Germans responded to the attack "with their accustomed speed and efficiency." Lord Mountbatten, on the other hand, told Churchill that the Germans had been "rattled" by the raid, and that the lessons from the raid would be "invaluable" for planning a cross-Channel invasion.

Churchill was initially satisfied by Mountbatten's report and did not learn until many weeks later that the raid had been a costly fiasco. His frustration bubbled out in subsequent queries to his service chiefs, in which he complained that "everyone was concerned to make this business look as good as possible." As Hastings summarizes, "leaders and planners had failed at every level.... It is scant wonder that Churchill lacked confidence in his commanders, and remained morbidly fearful that Britain's war-making instruments were doomed to break in his hand." The poor showing at Dieppe contributed to the decision to postpone Overlord from 1943 to 1944.

As D-Day approached, it became increasingly evident that the numerically superior American forces would bear the heaviest burden of the landings, and Churchill had come to appreciate the competence of the supreme allied commander, General Eisenhower. Still Churchill fretted. He candidly expressed his fears about Overlord to Eisenhower: "When I think of the beaches of Normandy choked with the flowers of American and British youth and when, in my mind's eye, I see the tides running red with blood, I have my doubts, Ike. I have my doubts." He worried further about every logistical detail of such an unprecedented undertaking, from the number of troops, the number and availability of landing craft, the problem of harbors and logistics (at least twelve thousand tons of supplies would need to be offloaded each day, Churchill calculated), and the weather. "The fools or knaves who had chalked 'Second Front Now' on our walls for the past two years had not had their minds burdened by such problems. I had long pondered upon them."

But even the steadily growing capacities of the invasion force (aided, not incidentally, by Churchill's initiatives to develop "new engines of war" specially for the landing, such as the artificial concrete harbors codenamed "mulberries") did not relieve Churchill's third major concern about the D-Day plan, which was purely political.

Already by 1943 Churchill was concerned about the shape of the post-war world—namely, that the Soviet Union might dominate most or all of Europe unless the Western allies (the U.S., Britain, and France) successfully cut off the Soviet advance. One of Churchill's greatest frustrations with the United States as the war proceeded was the failure of the American leadership to see the outline of the Cold War to come. On his way to the Tehran summit in 1943, Churchill told Harold Macmillan, "Germany is finished.... The real problem now is Russia. I can't get the Americans to see it." As Churchill put the matter to Eisenhower in 1945, "I deem it highly important that we should shake hands with the Russians as far to the East as possible."

Churchill, therefore, proposed that the Western allies invade Europe through the Mediterranean and drive toward Germany from the south. This strategy might be thought of as an early version of "containment," a policy that would be pursued several years later— too late for Eastern Europe. The Allies were already slogging up the Italian peninsula, an effort that had to be scaled back to gather the forces for Overlord. Churchill thought Turkey might be brought into the war on the Allies' side (in contrast to its alignment in the previous war) if his strategy were followed. His critics thought he was trying to re-enact and vindicate the eastern strategy from World War I that had led, through little fault of Churchill's, to the disaster at Gallipoli. But he was never able to persuade the United States of the virtues of his strategic outlook.

Despite declaring in May 1945 that "I am hardening to this enterprise," Churchill still had his doubts that Overlord would fulfill its planners' hopes. This was especially true of General Bernard Montgomery, whom Churchill held in light regard. Montgomery boasted in planning meetings, "When D-Day ends, I will be knocking at the very outskirts of Caen." It took "Monty" more than a month to secure Caen.

Churchill had said to Eisenhower at a Downing Street luncheon around that time, "General, it's good for commanders to be optimistic, else they would never win a battle, but I must say to you that if, by the time snow flies, you have established your armies in Brittany on the Normandy coast and have the part of Cherbourg firmly in your grasp, I will be the first to congratulate you on a wonderfully conducted military campaign." Churchill added, "If, in addition, you have seized the port of Le Havre and have extended your holdings to include all the area, including the Cotentin Peninsula and the mouth of the Seine, I will proclaim that this is one of the finest operations in modern war."

"And finally," expanded Churchill, "if, by Christmas, you have succeeded in liberating our beloved Paris—if she can, by that time, regain her life of freedom and take her accustomed place as a center of Western European culture and beauty, then I will proclaim that this operation is the most grandly conceived and best conducted campaign in all history."

In typical Churchill fashion, as D-Day grew nearer, Churchill's hope and determination overcame his doubts. In the last planning meeting, Churchill asked to be allowed to watch the invasion from a navy ship offshore, and to embark briefly on one of the landing beaches. King George himself had to intervene to dissuade the prime minister. On June 5, it was the military commanders who had to check Churchill's enthusiasm and expectations. Admiral Andrew Cunningham came from a meeting with Churchill and recorded in his diary, "He really is an incorrigible optimist." And army chief of staff Alan Brooke wrote in his diary, "I found him over-optimistic as regards prospects of the cross-Channel operation, and tried to damp him down a bit."

Churchill's late enthusiasm turned out to be fully justified, of course. Though he originally misjudged the soundness of the D-Day plans, his characteristic prodding and argumentation actually contributed to the success of the invasion. Churchill was glad to be proved wrong.

CHAPTER 21

DREAMS OF DEFEAT

CHURCHILL'S PREMONITIONS HE WOULD LOSE THE ELECTION

When I give talks on Churchill across the country, the first question I am asked is invariably "Why did Churchill lose the election in 1945?" Indeed, when the British cast him out of office weeks after the final triumph over Hitler, people around the globe were aghast. The most famous personality and most popular hero in the world had been turned out by his people after leading them to victory over Germany in the greatest war in history. Even in Britain, where newspapers were closely following the course of the ten-week campaign in the early summer of that year, political reporters and polling groups were stunned. Yet there was one person in Britain who was not totally surprised: Churchill himself. He had had premonitions of his defeat in a pair of dreams that disturbed his usually sound sleep.

Churchill's defeat is often incomprehensible to Americans because of their unfamiliarity with British parliamentary elections, in which no one casts a ballot directly for prime minister as Americans do for president. Churchill's name did not appear on the ballots of most voters in Britain—only the voters in his Parliamentary constituency of Woodford had the opportunity to vote for or against him. The election of the British prime minister is a party affair—the party that wins a majority forms the government and names the prime minister. Americans are used to what is called "divided government"—a president of one party and a congressional majority of the other party. Divided government is impossible in a parliamentary system. Sometimes I have explained to audiences, "In 1956, President Eisenhower won re-election in a landslide. Yet, a majority Democratic Congress was elected at the same time. If we had Britain's parliamentary election system, the Democratic speaker of the House, Sam Rayburn, would have become the head of government." In a parliamentary system, personal popularity is not enough. Indeed, his opponents in the 1945 election occasionally implied that Churchill could somehow be kept on, a fact which Churchill noted in his final campaign broadcast on June 30:

> There is no truth in stories now being put about that you can vote for my opponents at this election, whether they be Labour or Liberal, without at the same time voting for my dismissal from power. This you should not hesitate to do if you think it right and best for the country. All that I ask is that you do it with your eyes open.

But there is more to this story than the peculiarities of the British electoral system. There is a useful lesson about partisan politics and perhaps the limits of partisan campaign rhetoric. On VE Day, May 8,

1945, when the prime minister stood with King George VI on the balcony of Buckingham Palace acknowledging the jubilant cheers of over a hundred thousand Londoners, his personal popularity could not have been higher. The approval ratings of both the sovereign and the head of his government approached 90 percent.

Churchill wanted to carry on the coalition government with the Labour Party until the war with Japan had ended in a similar victory. The Labour Party had entered the coalition in May 1940 with the agreement that once the war with Germany ended, the coalition would be dissolved and a general election would be called. While the Labour leader, Clement Attlee, was agreeable to Churchill's proposal to carry on until Japan capitulated, the rank and file of his party were not, so Churchill agreed to call an election. As Parliament adjourned for electioneering in their constituencies that May, Churchill's defeat was considered impossible. A scant six weeks later, however, Churchill was thrown out of office in a massive rejection of him and his party in favor of Attlee and Labour. Something happened in the mind of the majority of voters during that interval. As Paul Addison, the pre-eminent scholar of Churchill's domestic political career, has observed, "the general election of 1945 was the last election in which politicians on all sides relied mainly on guesswork and placed little reliance on the allegedly more scientific method of opinion polls in predicting the result." In fact, the Gallup poll had shown a consistent Labour lead over the Conservatives since at least 1942.

Churchill and his party did not fully grasp what was foremost in the minds of many British voters at the end of the war in Europe. First, the public rightly blamed Churchill's own party, the Conservatives, for having left the nation vulnerable to Germany in the late 1930s by its neglect of defense and its disastrous policy of appeasement. It did his party little good that Churchill had been its chief critic during his own "wilderness years." Second, the British people were tired of the privations of the war—food rationing, poor housing, and so forth—and were receptive to the platform of the Labour Party, which promised a return to an economy of prosperity and plenty through socialist policies such as nationalized industry and "free" health care.

Churchill assumed that his record in leading the nation to victory would be enough. Yet, for all of Churchill's skill in prognostication, he was less sure-footed in the gritty exigencies of practical politics and campaign tactics.

Furthermore, Churchill could not fully focus on the election campaign. From the heady realm of statecraft and diplomacy, he had now descended to the grubby arena of hard-knuckled politics. Issues had turned from the international to the domestic. A week before, he had been speaking about plans to organize the United Nations. Now he was talking about programs to set up a new health care insurance system. The switch from diplomacy to dentures not only slowed his mind but sapped his energies.

Now, in response to Labour's visionary plans for a welfare state, for new worker benefits, hospital care, and public housing, Conservatives were compelled to offer some generalized promises to counter them. What they came up with, however, was little more than lip service.

The Tories' election strategy would be centered not on a program but a person—Winston Churchill, the most recognized, most popular figure in the world. For local party chairmen, old resentments were shoved aside. Churchill was their trump card, and the candidates in their respective constituencies would ride his coattails to victory. He was their premier drawing card. Chairmen all over the country were vying with each other for Churchill's appearance in their town. No one, save King George himself, would attract a larger crowd.

For the election, the Conservatives had changed their name to National—which had been the designation of the coalition government during the war. Conservative campaign posters featured the face of Churchill and the slogan "Help Him Finish the Job: VOTE NATIONAL." Labour posters depicted an old, balding man with glasses with the words, "LABOUR FOR THE FUTURE." Another poster showed only a hand chained to a post with the line "INDUS-TRY MUST SERVE THE PEOPLE NOT ENSLAVE THEM."

All the attention on Churchill revealed not the strength of the Conservative Party but its weakness. Churchill's daughter Sarah offered a perceptive warning of the defects of the Tory strategy, noting that the people she talked to would not be "voting for Labour for their proclaimed ideals or beliefs but simply because life has been hard for them, often an unequal struggle, and they think that only by voting Labour will their daily struggle become easier." With no substantial program of his own to offer, Churchill's attacks on the Labour Party, though spirited, were probably counterproductive.

His most famous—some say infamous—attack on the Labour Party was his so-called "Gestapo" speech, in which he charged,

> No Socialist government conducting the entire life and industry of the country could afford to allow free, sharp, or violently worded expressions of public discontent. They would have to fall back on some form of Gestapo.

Churchill went on to explain:

> ... Socialism would gather all power to the supreme party and party leaders, rising like stately pinnacles above their vast bureaucracies of civil servants no longer servants, no longer civil.

Churchill could envision the total welfare state that the Labour pamphlets were promising: "the state would be the arch-employer, the arch-planner, the arch-administrator, and ruler and the arch-caucus boss." In that sort of state monopoly, Churchill could well imagine officious bureaucrats evolving into some sort of "political police."

When his wife and daughter read a draft of the speech, they both begged him to remove the "Gestapo" reference, but Churchill refused. Yet the critics within his own household were right: the reference to the most odious aspect of the recently defeated enemy struck a discordant note. Churchill had worked with socialists like Attlee and Ernest Bevin in the coalition government. He admired them and knew they respected human liberties and loathed the kind of personality cult that Hitler and Stalin promoted. Churchill's speech attracted fierce criticism from the press and was bitterly resented by his Labour opponents. It cannot be proved that the word "Gestapo" caused his defeat, but it unquestionably contributed to it.

Churchill delivered his notorious speech not long before the Potsdam Conference, where he would meet in early July with Stalin and the new American president, Harry Truman. Churchill, head of the caretaker government until the results of the election were known, announced to the House of Commons that Attlee would accompany him to Potsdam. A Labour MP jeered, "Is the Right Honourable Gentleman going to take the Gestapo with him?"

It was not the high-ranking Labour Members in the Commons that worried Churchill, not even the fire-eating Welshman Aneurin Bevan, who had continually sniped at him during the war. What worried him were the heads of the trade unions, particularly the head of the electrical union, who was an outright Communist. They crafted the new programs with the help of their Marxist allies in the universities. The rank and file of the Labour movement followed their dictates.

Churchill tried to get his campaign back on track to rally Conservatives. He ended his first campaign speech with:

> On with the forward march! Leave the Socialist dreamers
> to their Utopias or their nightmares. Let us be content to

do the heavy job that is right on top of us. And let us make sure that the cottage home to which the warrior will return is blessed with modest but solid prosperity, well-fenced, and guarded against misfortunes, and that Britons remain free to plan their lives for themselves and for those they love.

During his series of speaking stops in the north, Churchill was mobbed by crowds waving "Good old Winnie" and "V-for-victory" signs. Local party officials said his radio talk had been a winner. But his doctor, Charles Moran, said later that "he didn't seem to have the old vim. The words were right, but his heart wasn't in it."

The Labour Party was increasingly confident that it would make gains in the new Parliament. Nevertheless, winning a majority seemed a long shot, considering the sizable majority of seats the Conservatives had held since 1940. From that time, the continuance of the coalition government precluded elections except in the case of a Member's death. Additionally, most of the Conservative Members had been serving since the early 1930s and enjoyed the power of incumbency. The familiarity of their names and their faithful service to their constituents, such as finding out more about the whereabouts of their military sons fighting abroad or handling some mix-up in a claim to the government, were also in the Conservatives' favor.

Yet Churchill had a sense that he was running against the clock— that the momentum might be shifting to Labour. The soundings and surveys, however, all pointed to a Conservative victory, though with a reduced majority.

On July 5, the country voted. Results would not be known for three weeks, because the votes from the army, navy, and air force had to be submitted from afar.

Churchill took his first holiday in years in Bordeaux, France, and then flew to Potsdam. There Stalin reported to Churchill that his embassy in London had predicted that Conservatives would end up with an eighty-seat majority. Coincidentally, Churchill's son, Randolph, made the same prediction.

Both the foreign secretary, Anthony Eden, and Churchill's personal aide, John Peak, thought the prime minister was off his form in the meetings with Truman and Stalin. On one of the nights at the villa in Potsdam, he woke from a troubling nightmare. "I had an unpleasant dream," he told his doctor, Lord Moran. "I dreamed that life was over. I was on a gurney in a hospital, my dead body under a white sheet on a table in an empty room. I recognized my bare feet projecting from under the sheet." He sensed this was a foreboding of defeat: "Perhaps this is the end." It was not his last such premonition.

When Churchill arrived back in London, he heard reports that Labour headquarters was predicting a thirty-seat Conservative margin. His own people were tripling that estimate. Churchill went to bed the night before the election returns were to be counted confident once again that he was going to be returned to power. In the final volume of his World War II memoirs, *Triumph and Tragedy*, Churchill described the next morning:

> However, just before dawn I woke suddenly with a sharp stab of almost physical pain. A hitherto subconscious conviction that we were beaten broke forth and dominated my mind. All the pressure of great events, on and against which I had mentally so long maintained my "flying speed," would cease and I should fail. The power to shape the future would be denied me. The knowledge and experience I had gathered, the authority and goodwill I had gained in so many countries, would vanish. I was discontented at the prospect, and turned over at once to sleep again.

Yet this grim prospect was exactly what unfolded over the next twenty-four hours. Churchill waited for returns with his daughter Sarah and brother Jack in the Map Room of the underground annex at 10 Downing Street. The results staggered him. At 1:00 a.m. the BBC announced a Labour landslide. With 393 seats, Labour had a majority of 146 seats over all other parties.

Churchill's wife and Mary, his daughter, came down from Woodford to console him. "It could be a blessing in disguise," Clementine said.

"If so, it is certainly well disguised," was his droll reply.

Despite this crushing defeat, Churchill's great career was not yet finished, even though he was seventy years old at this point. One of his favorite maxims from his ancestor, the first duke of Marlborough, was, "As I think most things are settled by destiny, when one has done one's best, the only thing is to await the result with patience." And so his next act of political prophecy was that he would be prime minister again. While most observers thought his political career was at last over, he told a secretary: "I know I am going to be prime minister again. I know it." And he was, starting in 1951.

PART VI

THE COLD WAR

CHAPTER 22

THE IRON CURTAIN WARNING

CHURCHILL DENOUNCES SOVIET RUSSIA

Churchill's "Iron Curtain" speech at Fulton, Missouri, on March 5, 1946, ranks as one of the most famous and consequential speeches ever made by someone out of high office, comparable in its force to Lincoln's "House Divided" speech of 1858 and Martin Luther King's "I Have a Dream" speech of 1963. It is remembered as the announcement to the world of the beginning of the Cold War, although as Churchill knew the seeds had been germinating for some time. It crystallized the new situation facing the United States and Western democracies and also forecast how the new and unusual "cold" war should be conducted so as to avoid World War III and achieve a peaceful future.

As we saw, Churchill had difficulty getting the U.S. government to look ahead to the potential political difficulties with the Soviet

Union after the war. He remarked to Franklin Roosevelt shortly before the Yalta summit in February 1945, "At the present time I think the end of this war may well prove to be more disappointing than was the last." Churchill's great fear as he traveled to the United States in early 1946 was that the Western democracies would repeat the same mistakes that had so nearly cost them their lives a decade before. As he wrote in *The Gathering Storm*, the Western democracies "need only to repeat the same well-meaning, short-sighted behavior towards the new problems which in singular resemblance confront us today to bring about a third convulsion from which none may live to tell the tale."

Although President Harry Truman quickly took the measure of the Soviet Union, it was not yet clear whether the United States would embrace a role as the leader of the free world or would link arms with Britain and other Western European nations in a defensive alliance against the Soviet Union. The status and intentions of Soviet forces in Iran and Eastern Europe were uncertain. There was the prospect of Communist takeovers of the governments of France, Italy, and Spain. America was rapidly demobilizing after the victory over Japan barely six months before, and Americans were looking forward to the material blessings of peace. Churchill knew his warning would cast a pall over the mood of the nation.

Truman might have understood the dark intentions of the Soviet Union, but many leading American liberals, such as FDR's former vice president, Henry Wallace, and his widow, Eleanor Roosevelt, still affectionately referred to the Communist dictator Stalin as "good old Uncle Joe." It was difficult for Americans, in the space of a few months, to go from regarding the Soviet Union as our ally in war to a potentially lethal enemy. Much of the liberal press was trying to drive a wedge between the U.S. and Britain, while rightwing isolationists opposed any long-term American alliance with European nations.

In the midst of these powerful political crosscurrents, Churchill's Iron Curtain address prepared the way for the NATO alliance and a Western plan for defense against Soviet encroachment.

The term "Iron Curtain" defined the Soviet tyranny that extended its grasp over Eastern Europe. Although the public came to know the phrase from Churchill's Fulton speech, he had first used it in a telegram to Truman the preceding May, days after the German surrender but before the two leaders met for the first time at the Potsdam conference. "I am profoundly concerned about the European situation," Churchill wrote. "An iron curtain is being drawn down upon their front," he wrote of the Soviet forces settling down in Eastern European nations. "We do not know what is going on behind.... Meanwhile the attention of our peoples will be occupied in inflicting severities on Germany, which is ruined and prostrate, and it would be open to the Russians in a very short time to advance if they chose to the waters of the North Sea and the Atlantic."

While Churchill is often credited with having originated the phrase "iron curtain," he may, ironically enough, have gotten the term from Count Schwerin von Krosigk, the foreign minister of Germany in the last days of the war, who, the *Times* reported, had warned in a radio broadcast a few days before VE Day, "In the East the iron curtain behind which, unseen by the eyes of the world, the work of destruction goes on, is moving steadily forward."[1]

Regardless of the origin of the phrase, Churchill had been looking ahead to this problem since early in the war. In 1970, the retired prime minister Harold Macmillan related to the thirty-year-old Winston Churchill II a conversation he had had with the young man's grandfather in early 1942. "It was after a dinner hosted by General Eisenhower for the joint Anglo-American command in Algiers, and your grandfather asked me to come back to his room for a drink. 'What type of man do you think Cromwell is?' was his odd question to me.

I uttered, 'Very aggressive, wasn't he?' Your grandfather looked at me gravely and said, 'Cromwell was obsessed with Spain but never saw the danger of France.'"

"At that time," continued Macmillan to the younger Churchill, "we were losing the war, but with America now in, Churchill had concluded totalitarian Nazism would be defeated and totalitarian Communism would take its place as the threat to Europe and the world."

Churchill had declined a steady stream of high-profile speaking invitations in the first months after the war, including those from the kings and queens of Norway, Denmark, and Holland, as well as from Canada and Australia. "I refuse," said Churchill, "to be exhibited like a prize bull whose chief attraction is his past prowess." But Churchill could hardly turn down an invitation than came from the White House in September 1945. Churchill opened it and saw that it was an invitation to speak at Westminster College in a town he had never heard of. Scoffing, he threw it down and said, "I supposed colleges in America are too named 'Parliament.'" But his daughter Sarah read it and saw that there was a postscript at the bottom of the invitation. "This is a wonderful school in my home state. Hope you can do it. I'll introduce you. s/g Harry Truman."

An introduction by the president of the United States would afford Churchill a world stage—whatever the venue. Though the date of the address, March 5, 1946, was half a year away, the opportunity fueled his imagination. He may have been out of office, but he was still the world's foremost political figure, a man whose words could still command attention in the world's leading nation. The thought buoyed his spirit, as he resumed his role of Leader of the Opposition.

In February, Churchill, accompanied by Sarah, sailed on the *Queen Elizabeth* to New York and then took a train to Miami, where a Montreal friend had lent him his home for some sun and sand before meeting President Truman in Washington.

During the five-day cruise, Churchill had worked on his Westminster College address, using notes he had made in London. His grandson has told me that Churchill would spend an hour for every minute in an address. On this address, Churchill would triple that time.

In Miami, Churchill completed his first draft, writing mostly on the sunny terrace outside the living room. During his stay, he spoke on the need for Anglo-American unity at the University of Miami, where, after receiving his honorary doctorate, he made this comment: "Perhaps no one has ever passed so few examinations and received so many degrees."

On the last day of February, Churchill took a sleeper to Washington, D.C., where he holed up in the British embassy, editing his address, which he decided to title "The Sinews of Peace," a play on Cicero's adage "Nervos belli, pecuniam infinitam" ("The sinews of war are endless money").

Churchill was striking his familiar theme that only preparedness could ensure peace. The Soviet political and military encroachments could be stopped only by a united West under the resolute leadership of the United States. He wanted to shake America out of the game of intellectual make-believe that engendered its cozy confidence in the United Nations. The mask of democratic pretension had to be ripped from the Kremlin's face and its imperialism revealed. Churchill saw it as his duty to dispel Washington's illusion (shared by London) that it was at peace with its former Soviet ally.

By coincidence, a few days before Churchill arrived in Washington, George Kennan dispatched his famous "long telegram" from Moscow. Clarifying the nature and strategy of the Soviet Union and closely tracking Churchill's views, Kennan's report became the cornerstone of the "containment" doctrine. The Soviet threat, he wrote, "will really depend on the degree of cohesion, firmness and vigor which [the] Western World can muster. And this is [the] factor which it is within our power to influence." Kennan's message attracted

considerable attention within the highest reaches of the U.S. government. Churchill, unaware of the secret telegram, could hardly have
asked for a better prologue for his Fulton message.

As a political courtesy, Churchill called the White House and
inquired if the president wanted to look over a draft of his Fulton
speech. The White House replied that Under Secretary of State Dean
Acheson would instead call at the British embassy. Lester Pearson, the
Canadian ambassador, had already told Churchill that Acheson not
only had a sound diplomatic head but also had a keen ear for the
elegant phrase.

The tall, elegant, and mustached Acheson must have reminded
Churchill of his own foreign minister Anthony Eden. Churchill greeted
the under secretary in his green dragon dressing gown. Acheson had
two suggestions for the speech. First, eliminate the reference to World
War II as "the unnecessary war," which he thought rightwing Republicans would seize upon to justify their opposition to Roosevelt and
their continuing isolationism. Second, include some praise for the
United Nations as a peacekeeping instrument. When Acheson left,
Churchill acceded to the advice. He also showed the speech to Secretary of State James Byrnes, who, Churchill reported, "was excited
about it and did not suggest any alterations."

On March 4, Churchill joined the presidential party aboard the
Ferdinand Magellan (the train specially built in 1939 to accommodate
presidential security and Roosevelt's wheelchair) at Washington's
Union Station. When Truman noticed Churchill studying the presidential seal on the train, he proudly pointed out a change he had made
to the seal—the eagle now turned to face the olive branch instead of
the arrows. Churchill knew that his speech the next day might dissi-
pate some of the rosy glow of the immediate postwar peace and he
could not quite give the new seal his full approval. He asked the
president, "Why not put the eagle's neck on a swivel so that it could
turn to the right or left as the occasion presented itself?"

On the train, Churchill finally shared a draft of his Fulton speech with Truman, who expressed his approval. "He told me he thought it was admirable," Churchill later wrote, after Truman had distanced himself from the speech, "and would do nothing but good, though it would make a stir." That it certainly did.

During the journey, Churchill continued to make more changes and corrections to his draft, even though an embargoed text had already been forwarded to press offices and chanceries around the world. In his "Scaffolding of Rhetoric"—notes on the art of speaking that he had written almost half a century earlier—Churchill had emphasized the necessity of a metaphor or image to give a picture to an abstraction. In his draft, Churchill had mentioned "tyranny," "imperialism," and "totalitarian systems," but those words lacked imagery that would stick in his audience's mind.

Late that night in his stateroom, Churchill surveyed a map of Europe, drawing a black line from the Baltic states to Trieste. By one report, it was then that Churchill added the phrase for which his speech would be known. When the train made its only stop for refueling, Churchill lifted his curtain and saw that they were in Springfield, Illinois, "the home of Lincoln." Sentimentalists like to believe that the ghost of that other champion of freedom and master of the English language inspired him.

The train stopped at the St. Louis station in the early morning of March 5. Churchill took a leisurely breakfast in his stateroom before he and the presidential party switched to a local train for Jefferson City. There, Churchill and Truman entered their open-car limousines for the motorcade into Fulton. Churchill found, to his dismay, that he was lacking the requisite prop—a cigar. So he stopped at a local tobacconist for the purchase.

After lunch at the home of Westminster's president, Churchill was taken to the college gymnasium for his speech. In his introduction, President Truman was characteristically plainspoken: "Mr. Churchill and I believe in freedom of speech. I understand Mr. Churchill might have something useful and constructive to say."

Typically, Churchill opened on a light but warm note that immediately won the affection of his audience. With his hands clasping his honorary academic robes, he peered over his black spectacles and harrumphed in his habitual stuttering style:

> I am glad to come to Westminster College... the name Westminster is somehow familiar to me. I seem to have heard of it before. Indeed, it was at Westminster that I received a very large part of my education.

Then with his palms upturned, as if he was stripped of power, Churchill offered a disclaimer that anticipated the cool reception his speech would receive in official Washington and London: "Let me... make it clear that I have no official mission of any kind and that I speak only for myself."

He continued by stating that the paramount mission facing the world was the prevention of another global war. Raising his forefinger twice in emphasis, he pointed to two institutions with major roles in the maintenance of peace: the United Nations and the continuing "special relationship" between Britain and America. "The United Nations," he said, "must be a reality and not a sham, and not some cockpit in a Tower of Babel."

Then, with Miltonic foreboding, Churchill began his celebrated description of postwar Europe: "A shadow has fallen upon the scenes so lately lighted by the Allied victory." Then with clenched fist, he sketched the cause of that darkness in the paragraph he had added on the train, beginning with this internal rhyme:

> From Stettin in the Baltic to Trieste in the Adriatic an iron curtain has descended across the continent. Behind that line

lie all the capitals of the ancient states of Central and Eastern Europe: Warsaw, Berlin, Prague, Vienna, Belgrade,
Bucharest, and Sofia. All of these famous cities and the
populations lie in what I must call the Soviet sphere....

At this point the public address system malfunctioned, but a former
army radio technician in uniform sitting under the head table pushed
his way through his fellow veterans to find the wire, which he then
held to restore the amplification. (Churchill later recorded the speech
in its entirety.) The *Washington Post* reporter, Ed Folliard, who followed only the advance text of the speech, failed to mention the "iron
curtain" paragraph in the next day's paper.

Churchill then offered insight into the mind of the Kremlin that
would not be matched until the days of Ronald Reagan: "I do not
believe that Soviet Russia desires war. What they desire is the fruits
of war and the indefinite expansion of powers and doctrines." For
such Soviet imperialism, he offered this prescription:

From what I have seen of our Russian friends and Allies
during the war, I am convinced that there is nothing they
admire so much as strength, and there is nothing for which
they have less respect than for weakness, especially military
weakness.

Then he reinforced his postwar call for action with a reminder of his
unheeded warnings before the war:

Last time I saw it all coming and cried aloud to my fellow
countrymen and the world, but no one paid attention. Up
to the year 1933 or even 1935, Germany might have been
saved from the awful fate which had overtaken her, and
we might have been spared the miseries Hitler let loose

upon mankind. There was never a war in all history easier
to prevent by timely action than the one which has just
desolated such great areas of the globe. It could have been
prevented, in my belief, without the firing of a single shot,
and Germany might be powerful, prosperous, and honored
today; but no one would listen, and one by one we were all
sucked into the awful whirlpool.

Churchill's reception reflected his audience's recognition that a great
leader had honored their town and college with his visit rather than
their appreciation of the stern message. In Washington and around
the world, the speech precipitated a storm of denunciation. Both Truman and Attlee took shelter by disowning Churchill's message; Truman denied that he had any foreknowledge of what Churchill was
going to say.

From the Kremlin, Stalin exploded with rage in a cable. Truman,
in response, invited him to come to Fulton or Washington to deliver
his response. Truman also offered to send the USS *Missouri* (on which
Japan had surrendered) to bring him to America. There was no reply.
Three Democratic senators called a press conference in the capitol to
condemn the speech as "shocking." Eleanor Roosevelt accused
Churchill of being a "warmonger" and risking a World War III.

Churchill himself felt his speech had failed in its purpose to arouse
public opinion against Stalinism. Even the conservative *Wall Street
Journal* demurred: "The United States wants no alliance against
Russia." The left was harsher. The *Nation* said Churchill had added
a sizable bit of poison to the deteriorating relations. Nobel Prize–
winning author Pearl Buck concluded, "We are now nearer war."

Churchill returned to Washington. A few days later, he was offered
some solace by General Eisenhower, who put him up at Fort Myers.
According to Eisenhower's grandson, Eisenhower applauded the message. The new army chief of staff defended his boss, arguing that

Truman privately agreed with Churchill's assessment but wanted Churchill to do the heavy lifting. Truman, Eisenhower explained, was fearful of his chances not only for re-election but even for re-nomination. At Potsdam, Truman had offered Eisenhower the Democratic nomination for the presidency, with Truman as his running mate. Eisenhower turned him down.

Truman was not assured of his party's nomination. The left wing, led by Henry Wallace, was championing peace and friendship with Russia, while there were rumors of the conservative Southern Democrats looking for a more probable winner.

Yet as Eisenhower had assured him, Truman shared Churchill's conviction regarding the Soviet threat. Days later, protests were delivered to Moscow concerning Soviet actions in Iran and Eastern Europe. Thus ended the era guided by Roosevelt's blind trust in Russia.

If at first Western ears were deaf to the shuddering clang of the iron curtain's descent, they would soon hear its echo. The free world would remember Churchill's warning. Truman, to his credit, after his unexpected victory in 1948 initiated the North Atlantic Treaty Alliance, declared the Truman Doctrine aiding Greece in its war against Communist guerrillas, and implemented the Marshall plan for the economic and industrial recovery of Europe.

Recognizing the nature of the Soviet regime and the need to counter it through a resolute Western alliance was but the first of Churchill's prescient warnings about the postwar world. He soon offered three more insights that proved essential to winning the Cold War almost forty years later.

CHAPTER 23

BLOODSHED AVERTED

HE PREDICTS WORLD WAR III WILL BE AVERTED

Churchill's historical perspective shaped many of his perceptions and predictions of world affairs, but equally important in forming his views were "new facts." And the most decisive new fact of the Cold War era that followed World War II was the atomic bomb and its more powerful successor, the hydrogen bomb. The original ten- to fifteen-kiloton scale of atomic warheads, such as those used at Hiroshima and Nagasaki, did not strike Churchill as exceptional; conventional area-bombing late in the war had been just as destructive.

"The atomic bomb," he told the House of Commons in the mid-1950s, "with all its terrors, did not carry us outside the scope of human control or manageable events in thought or action, in peace or war." But the much larger hydrogen bomb, with its megaton yields, was another matter. With the creation of an arsenal of warheads of this size, "the entire foundation of human affairs was revolutionized, and mankind placed in a situation both measureless and laden with doom." Churchill's prophecy from his 1924 essay "Shall We All Commit Suicide?" appeared to have come to pass: "Without having improved appreciably in virtue or enjoying wiser guidance, [mankind] has got into its hands for the first time the tools by which it can unfailingly accomplish its own extermination."

But Churchill was neither a pessimist nor a fatalist. To the contrary, he predicted that there would be no World War III. He agreed that, in the abstract, the best solution would be "bona fide disarmament all around." But he also knew this was unrealistic; the Soviet Union was not amenable to "an effective system of inspection," which would be necessary for a real disarmament agreement to be reached. Instead, Churchill settled early upon the extreme form of deterrence that was officially embraced as strategic doctrine in the 1960s: mutual assured destruction (or MAD). And while moralists on all sides abhorred the MAD doctrine, it formed the cornerstone of Churchill's belief that World War III would not be fought. Churchill deserves to be remembered as a principal architect of both the doctrine of containment (which he prescribed in the Iron Curtain speech) and its handmaiden, the doctrine of nuclear deterrence.

Churchill never used the phrase "mutual assured destruction." As usual, his language was richer and more colorful. "[I]t may well be that we shall by a process of sublime irony have reached a stage in this story where safety will be the sturdy child of terror, and survival the twin brother of annihilation.... Major war of the future will differ, therefore, from anything we have known in the past in this one significant respect; that each side, at the outset, will suffer what it dreads the most, the loss of everything that it has ever known."[1]

To be sure, Churchill thought there was some risk of a conventional war in Europe against the Soviet Union—if NATO were to neglect its own conventional defenses. Proper deterrence required both nuclear and regular forces, Churchill thought, along with diplomatic engagement with the Soviet Union. These were Churchill's chief objectives when he resumed the premiership in late 1951. In his first speech in the House after returning to 10 Downing Street, Churchill said, "Never must we admit that a Third World War is inevitable. I heard some months ago a foreign diplomatist who was asked, 'In which year do you think the danger of war will be the greatest?' He replied: 'Last year.'" On his first day in office, Churchill sent a telegram to Stalin offering an open door for negotiations to reduce Cold War tensions and proposing a resumption of the wartime "Big Three" summit meetings. Stalin was not interested. Neither was President Truman.

The key to everything, in Churchill's view, was the United States. Even though Truman was committed to NATO and embraced the strategy of containment and deterrence (most notably in the famous NSC-68 memorandum, written principally by Paul Nitze, calling for an aggressive anti-Soviet strategy), it was by no means clear, even as late as 1952, that the United States was in it for the long haul. There were still strong isolationist sentiments and some leading Republicans, including at times the 1952 potential presidential nominee, Senator Robert A. Taft, expressed doubts and opposition to long-term American commitment to European security. At a lunch about a month after his election, Churchill shared his thoughts on the prospect of war with a small circle of friends. If there were to be a war, John Colville recounted in his diary, Churchill thought it would come because the United States, unwilling to continue footing the bill for the military and economic recovery of Europe, might give an ultimatum to the Soviets to withdraw from Eastern Europe or face war. Or the Russians, seeing that Western Europe was rearming itself, could decide, strategically, that it was better to attack sooner rather than later. But Churchill viewed both possibilities as improbable. He could only hope to influence one of the superpowers, of course, so he naturally made plans to visit America as soon as he could. "If war comes,"

Churchill told the House shortly before departing for America, "it will be because of forces beyond British control. On the whole I do not think it will come."

Churchill had got on well with Truman both at Potsdam and after he had left the premiership in 1945, most notably at Fulton in 1946. Now that he was back in power, Churchill wanted to take up where they had left off. (At this point in early 1952, no one knew if Truman would stand for re-election or whether Dwight Eisenhower would run for the GOP nomination that year.)

Over five long meetings, Churchill and Truman worked their way patiently through a long list of issues concerning the Anglo-American-led alliance against the Soviet bloc and considered whether they should seek a summit meeting with Stalin or his successors. (Truman was unenthusiastic about a summit, both on the merits and because he feared criticism from Senator Joseph McCarthy and his allies.) Churchill discounted the possibility of a deliberate Soviet attack on Western Europe, but only if the architecture of NATO, led above all by the English-speaking nations, was firm.

The rhetorical centerpiece of his visit to the United States, however, was an address to a joint session of Congress, reminiscent of his dramatic address shortly after Pearl Harbor eleven years earlier. Building on his Iron Curtain speech of 1946, Churchill reinforced the importance of avoiding another world war through deterrence—especially including the deterrence of nuclear weapons:

> The vast process of American rearmament in which the British Commonwealth and Empire and the growing power of United Europe will play their part to the utmost of their strength, this vast process has already altered the balance of the world and may well, if we all persevere steadfastly and loyally together, avert the danger of a Third World War....

He then referred to the atomic bomb, which constituted "at present" the "supreme deterrent" against a third world war. He added this warning:

> If I may say this, Members of Congress, be careful above all things, therefore, not to let go of the atomic weapon until you are sure, and more than sure, that other means of preserving peace are in your hands. It is my belief that by accumulating deterrents of all kinds against aggression, we shall, in fact, ward off the fearful catastrophe, the fears of which darken the life and mar the progress of all the peoples of the globe.

A few months later Churchill repeated this argument to the new NATO supreme commander, General Matthew Ridgway, this time offering his firmest statement yet that there would be no Third World War:

> Let me tell you why, in my opinion, and it is only an opinion, not a prophecy, a Third World War is unlikely to happen. It is because, among other reasons, it would be entirely different in certain vital aspects from any other war that has ever taken place. Both sides know that it would begin with horrors of a kind and on a scale never dreamed of before by human beings. It would begin by both sides in Europe suffering in the first stage exactly what they dread the most.

Although Churchill emphasized the military aspects of deterrence, there were several other parts to his view about how World War III would be avoided—above all the reconciliation of Western Europe that had proved impossible, and subsequently poisonous, after World

War I. In his speech to Congress, Churchill noted that the Soviet challenge was, ironically, helping to promote the reconciliation and new unity of Western Europe after the war. In other words, the Soviet Union was strengthening the "special relationship" between the United States and the United Kingdom:

> There are, however, historic compensations for the stresses which we suffer in the 'cold war.' Under the pressure and menace of Communist aggression the fraternal association of the United States with Britain and the British Commonwealth, and the new unity growing up in Europe—nowhere more hopeful than between France and Germany—all these harmonies are being brought forward, perhaps by several generations in the destiny of the world. If this proves true— and it has certainly been proved true up to date—the architects of the Kremlin may be found to have built a different and a far better world than what they had planned.

But if the Soviet threat made European reconciliation possible, achieving a durable alliance against the Soviet Union would require more than the mere passing of historical enmities between nations and peoples, more than setting aside the desire for revenge and reparation. A higher degree of genuine political unity would be required, culminating in perhaps the most unthinkable act of all: the rapid rehabilitation of Germany as a great nation. To these related aspects of Churchill's foresight we now turn.

CHAPTER 24

THE "UNITED STATES OF EUROPE"

CHURCHILL FORESEES THE EUROPEAN UNION

Today European unity is an accepted fact, despite the prolonged economic crisis that has threatened the existence of the common currency, the euro, and despite the absence of the external threat of the Soviet Union, which was one of the preeminent causes of closer European cooperation in the postwar decades. Although it was widely believed after World War II that Europe had to break the centuries-long cycle of national conflicts, it was not clear that the increasingly formal political and economic integration of Europe was feasible or that the rapid rehabilitation of Germany was necessary for the project to succeed. Few people even considered the idea. Churchill, naturally, was among the first to do so. His approach to the problem of postwar Europe reflects his characteristic statesmanship.

Throughout the closing stages of World War II and in the immediate aftermath, two problems confronted the victorious Western Allies. First, there was the problem of rebuilding Europe's decimated economy. Solving this problem required solving the second problem: what to do about defeated Germany.

In 1946 and 1947, there were no signs of what later would become known as the "German economic miracle," the fruit of German finance minister Ludwig Erhard's courageous decisions to de-control most of Germany's economy. (Prior to Erhard's moves, Germans complained that British maladministration, imposed by the socialist government that succeeded Churchill in 1945, was doing more damage to Germany than the wartime bombing.) Erhard's reforms, however, did not take place until 1948. In 1946 and 1947, much of Europe, and especially Germany, was often close to starvation. The brutal winter of 1946–1947 aggravated already perilous conditions. Germany produced only about half as much food in 1947 as it had done in 1938. Millions were homeless. Western leaders worried about Communist revolution or victory in free elections. America's Marshall Plan, which began in 1947, helped to prevent complete catastrophe, but the long-term recovery of Europe needed more.

During the war Churchill had briefly expressed support for the notorious "Morgenthau Plan," named for Roosevelt's Treasury secretary, Henry Morgenthau Jr. At the second Quebec summit between FDR and Churchill in 1944, Morgenthau proposed that a defeated Germany should be "pastoralized"—its industrial capacity dismantled so completely that Germany would never be able to rearm and threaten war again. Initially Churchill "violently opposed this idea," as he put it in his memoirs, no doubt recalling the counterproductive results of the punitive terms of the Versailles Treaty after World War I, but he swung round to tentative support for the Morgenthau Plan under pressure from Roosevelt. He understood the logic: "We had

seen during the nineteen thirties how easy it was for a highly industrialized Germany to arm herself and threaten her neighbors,"
Churchill wrote in *Triumph and Tragedy*. But eventually even Roosevelt withdrew his support from Morgenthau's punitive proposal.
(Hitler skillfully exploited the Morgenthau Plan to motivate his
retreating army, telling Germans that the Allies intended to make
them slave laborers in a peasant economy.)

Still, the fear of an eventual return of German aggression was
inescapable. The revelations of the Holocaust and the other crimes
of the Nazis were still fresh in European minds. Churchill, though
out of office, was one of the first Western leaders to understand that
Germany needed to be rehabilitated both morally and economically
if Europe was to achieve a durable peace and prosperity. Only
Churchill could have urged that Germany be welcomed back into the
bosom of Europe right after World War II. Any other politician making such a recommendation would have risked obloquy or ostracism.
But the European statesman to whom the nations overrun by Hitler
owed their deliverance had to be given respectful consideration. For
Churchill, this was a message that had to be heard. No real recovery
of Europe could be achieved with the isolation of Germany.

Churchill's view was in keeping with the principle enunciated in
his six-volume memoir of World War II—"In war: resolution, in
defeat: defiance, in victory: magnanimity, in peace: good will"—as
well as his gracious attitude toward his prewar opponents during his
premiership: "If we open a quarrel between the present and the past,
we shall lose the future." Later, in 1952, Churchill told the *New York
Times*: "I always felt during the war that we must strike down the
tyrant, but be ready to help Germany up again as a friend."[1]

The key to a peaceful postwar Europe would be the relationship
between France and Germany. But this difficult rapprochement,
Churchill thought, required an even broader conception of European
unity. This he argued in perhaps his second-most famous postwar
speech (after the Iron Curtain speech in Fulton), which he delivered

in Zurich, Switzerland, in September 1946. In fact his grandson, Winston Churchill II, said that his grandfather considered the Zurich speech to rank second to Fulton in its importance for postwar history.

Surveying the gloomy postwar scene—"the tragedy of Europe"— Churchill warned that a new Dark Age, only narrowly averted through the help of the "great Republic across the Atlantic Ocean," might "still return." The victors are quarrelling; the vanquished suffering the "sullen silence of despair." "The guilty must be punished," he confirmed. "Germany must be deprived of the power to rearm and make another aggressive war. But when all this has been done, as it will be done, as it is being done, there must be an end to retribution."

Churchill had already previewed this much of his argument in a speech in the House of Commons shortly before traveling to Zurich: "Indescribable crimes had been committed by Germany under the Nazi rule. Justice must take its course, the guilty must be punished, but once that is over—and I trust it will soon be over—I fall back on the declaration of Edmund Burke, 'I cannot frame an indictment against an entire people.'" Now in Zurich he proposed the next step:

> Yet all the while there is a remedy which, if it were generally and spontaneously adopted, would as if by a miracle transform the whole scene, and would in a few years make all Europe, or the greater part of it, as free and as happy as Switzerland is today. What is this sovereign remedy? It is to re-create the European Family, or as much of it as we can, and provide it with a structure under which it can dwell in peace, in safety and in freedom. *We must build a kind of United States of Europe.* [Emphasis added.]

While describing a United States of Europe as a "federal system," Churchill did not specify how formal a political union there ought to be or whether this union required the modification of national sovereignty, as many present-day schemes of European unity do. Certainly Churchill's record and political philosophy suggest that he would be critical of the centralized bureaucracy growing in Brussels under today's European Union. He described his idea in vague and general terms, loosely analogous to, or compatible with, the newly established United Nations. He thought the project should start with some kind of European council: "The first step is to form a Council of Europe. If, at first, all the states of Europe are not willing or able to join the Union, we must nevertheless proceed to assemble and combine those that will or can."

The main rhetorical objective of the speech, however, was to gain general acceptance for the idea of European union, which a specific legal or constitutional proposal, such as today's Lisbon Treaty, would have undermined. Instead, he prepared his audience for the audacious heart of his message:

> I am now going to say something that will astonish you. The first step in the re-creation of the European family must be a partnership between France and Germany. In this way only can France recover the moral leadership of Europe. There can be no revival of Europe without a spiritually great France and a spiritually great Germany.

The idea of a more or less formal European political union did not originate with Churchill. In fact, he himself identified its antecedent as a proposal of the seventeenth-century French king Henry of Navarre for a pan-European council to mediate religious disputes.

Two years after Churchill's Zurich speech a conference was convened in The Hague to pursue the idea of European integration. To Churchill's great satisfaction, the conference included a German delegation. Although the conference was not an official diplomatic meeting of states (which is why Churchill, then out of power, could attend and take a leading role), it tried to build political momentum behind the idea of European unity. The conference was, as Churchill described it, a "Congress of a Europe striving to be reborn."

In his speech to The Hague, Churchill proposed going beyond a council, as he had suggested in Zurich, and establishing a European Assembly. Today's European Parliament in Strasbourg is such an assembly.

After the conference at The Hague, the first steps in European economic integration took place with the formation of the European Coal and Steel Community—the precursor to the Common Market of the 1960s, itself the precursor to the European Union in the 1990s. Step by step—a phrase Churchill used many times over his long career—European integration took shape, and another general war in the heart of Europe eventually became unimaginable.

Reconciliation between France and Germany was accomplished faster than perhaps even Churchill imagined under the leadership of the first elected postwar German chancellor, Konrad Adenauer, who worked productively with French foreign minister, Robert Schuman. Churchill later praised "their remarkable wisdom and their courage" in ending the centuries-old enmity between the two nations, and he called Adenauer "the wisest German statesman since the days of Bismarck." (On the occasion of his eightieth birthday, Churchill responded to Adenauer's birthday greetings, "I am high on the list of your admirers as a statesman and as a patriot.")

But Churchill judged rightly that his "United States of Europe" proposal with France and Germany at the center would "astonish." The London *Times* observed, "Churchill has proved again that he is not afraid to startle the world with new and even, as many must find them, 'outrageous propositions.'" The *Times*, which still had not got over his Fulton speech, missed the closing invitation of the Zurich speech in which Churchill expressed the hope that in the fullness of time perhaps the Soviet Union might be drawn into the United States of Europe. Instead the *Times* wrote: "He [Churchill] predicates his need for Germany in his scheme on the assumption that Europe is already irrevocably divided between East and West. That is the peril of his argument."

Here the *Times* completely misread Churchill. Not only did Churchill not regard the Cold War as "irrevocable," but he expressed the hope that the Soviet Union might join a unified Europe, a hope based on his parallel prediction that the Cold War would come to an end—a prediction that was even more astonishing than French-German reconciliation or the swift rise of European unity.

CHAPTER 25

THE END OF THE COLD WAR

HE PREDICTS THE IRON CURTAIN WILL FALL

Churchill's Cold War statecraft is often overlooked. He was out of power during the formative years of the Cold War, between 1945 and 1950. Even after he returned to 10 Downing Street from 1951 to 1955, Churchill was in a subordinate position to President Dwight Eisenhower. The Iron Curtain speech and Churchill's lifelong hostility to "Bolshevism" led many to assume that he was hostile to any negotiations with the Soviet Union and opposed to any form of détente. Yet he thought both were possible and indeed necessary. But his most audacious view was that the Cold War would end—and he even predicted when it would end, four decades in advance. He also predicted that China would not remain Communist, which arguably began to come true before Soviet Communism came to an end.

On New Year's Day 1953, Churchill remarked to his private secretary, John Colville, that if Colville lived a normal lifespan, he
"should assuredly see Eastern Europe free of Communism." Colville,
then thirty-eight years old, died in 1987 at the age of seventy-two, just
two years before the Berlin Wall came down and Eastern Europe
threw off Communist rule, and four years before the collapse of the
Soviet Union itself.

Churchill made this prediction just six weeks before Stalin died, a
time when few dared to hope that a third world war could be avoided,
much less that Communism could lose its grip on power. The lure of
Communist revolution was still strong in the developing world. But
as Churchill's comment to Colville makes clear, he perceived that the
challenge to Communism would come from the "captive nations" of
Eastern Europe. In an overlooked comment to Charles de Gaulle
shortly after the end of the Second World War, Churchill said that
while the Soviet Union was like a hungry wolf now, "after the meal
comes the digestion period." The USSR, he thought, would have a
difficult time "digesting" the peoples of Eastern Europe. His judgment was vindicated when the Soviet Union had to put down anti-
Communist uprisings in Hungary in 1956, Czechoslovakia in 1968,
and Poland in the 1980s—the Polish uprising being the one that
started the final unraveling of Communism.

And although Churchill did not clearly predict that the Soviet
Union itself might collapse as it did, he came close to suggesting that
a transformation or counterrevolution might be possible. On some
occasions he spoke hopefully about the possibility of a "spontaneous
and healthy evolution which may be taking place inside Russia." In
his 1949 speech at MIT, Churchill had the Soviet Union in mind when
he said,

> Laws just or unjust may govern men's actions. Tyrannies
> may restrain and regulate their words. The machinery of

propaganda may pack their minds with falsehoods and
deny them truth for many generations of time. But the soul
of man thus held in trance, or frozen in a long night, can
be awakened by a spark coming from God knows where,
and in a moment the whole structure of lies and oppression
is on trial for its life. Peoples in bondage need never despair.

In a 1952 speech to the U.S. Congress, Churchill said, "I am by no
means sure that China will remain for generations in the Communist
grip." The Korean War was then in a stalemate and unpopular with
the American people, but Churchill told President Truman that
June 25, 1950—the date of the UN resolution that marked America's
entry into the conflict—was the turning point in Communism's
danger to the free world.[1]

Churchill's hopeful expectation that Communism would not
endure contrasted sharply with the prevailing opinion, shared across
the political spectrum, that Communism was durable and that the
Soviet Union would be as permanent a fixture as the unified post-
Bismarck Germany. Many fellow-traveling leftists still thought Soviet-
style rule was the wave of the future; conservative pessimists feared
this was so, the most famous being Whittaker Chambers, the ex-spy
who thought he was joining "the losing side" when he broke with
Communism.

Even as Communism went into its death spiral in the 1980s,
Western intelligence continued to conclude that the Soviet Union was
robust and suffering from few serious weaknesses. As late as 1988,
barely a year before the fall of the Berlin Wall, the American foreign
policy establishment was still forecasting the long life of the Soviet
Union. Shortly after George H. W. Bush's election as president in
1988, State Department planners and academics from Harvard, Yale,
and Georgetown, along with other Sovietologists, met in Washington
to discuss relations with Moscow. Their consensus was that the Soviet

monolith and its satellite states in Eastern Europe and the Baltic would persist for the unforeseeable future—twenty, thirty, or even forty years.

Like many of Churchill's departures from the conventional wisdom, his prediction of the demise of Communism should be attributed not to clairvoyance but once again to his sense of history, combined with his instincts about the moral character of politics. While most modern observers of Communism regarded it as merely a bureaucratic variation of the ancient form of tyrannical rule, Churchill understood that Communism, unlike classical tyranny, was too contrary to human nature to endure. In other words, the state that Churchill once famously described as "a riddle wrapped in a mystery inside an enigma" was nonetheless not immune to politics and history. Churchill said as early as 1918 that Communism would fail because "it is fundamentally opposed to the needs and dictates of the human heart, and of human nature itself." He returned to this theme in 1957 when he wrote in a new edition of his World War II memoirs about the:

> complications and palliatives of human life that will render the schemes of Karl Marx more out of date and smaller in relation to world problems than they have ever been before. The natural forces are working with greater freedom and greater opportunity to fertilize and vary the thoughts and the power of individual men and women.... [I]n the main human society will grow in many forms not comprehended by a party machine.

Churchill would not have been surprised, I think, at the state of post-Soviet Russia. The authoritarianism to which it has reverted is quite different from the expansionist and ideologically utopian regime of Lenin and Stalin.

Churchill also thought he saw *how* the Cold War ought to come to an end, as well as *when*. Once again this "man of the past" would prove to be ahead of his time, as we shall see in the next chapter.

CHAPTER 26

"PARLEY AT THE SUMMIT"

CHURCHILL INVENTS "SUMMIT" MEETINGS

Throughout the Cold War, much hope was invested in the periodic "summit" meetings between the president of the United States and the general secretary of the Soviet Union. Always preceded by much fanfare, these meetings usually disappointed—until the very end of the Cold War, that is, when summits produced some dramatic breakthroughs. "Summits" and "summitry" became staples of both journalism and academia during this period. Few people recalled that the phrase originated with Churchill.

There had been meetings between heads of friendly countries many times before, of course (though not described by that term), notably during the Second World War, in which Churchill had played such a prominent role. Kings, emperors, prime ministers, and presidents had met to plan wars or to divide the spoils of war, as at the Congress of

Vienna after the Napoleonic wars and the Versailles Conference following World War I. But seldom had adversaries met in such a setting. Churchill's call for a high-level meeting between enemies during a Cold War seems surprising if one recalls that he was the most severe critic of the Cold War summits' closest historical precedent—the disastrous meeting at Munich between Chamberlain and Hitler, which produced the betrayal of Czechoslovakia.

Ironically enough, Churchill had called for just such a summit before World War II to unwind the mistakes of the Versailles Treaty. In 1933 Churchill said in a speech:

> I have spoken for years of a pyramid of peace, which might be triangular or quadrangular—three or four Great Powers shaking hands together and endeavouring to procure a rectification of some of the evils arising from the treaties made in the passion of war, which if left un-redressed will bring upon us consequences we cannot name....

Churchill felt that the aftermath of World War II—a divided Germany and Soviet domination of Eastern Europe—was as unsatisfactory and dangerous as the Versailles settlement had been. And now there was the specter of a nuclear arms race.

The idea that East-West differences could and should be worked out diplomatically appeared in Churchill's Iron Curtain speech but was obscured by the dramatic language about the Iron Curtain itself and the necessity of rearming the West. He had balanced the anti-Communism of his Fulton speech with the recognition of legitimate Soviet interests that the West should be willing to accommodate: "We understand the Russian need to be secure on her western frontiers by the removal of all possibility of German aggression. We welcome Russia to her rightful place among the leading nations of the world." "What is needed," he said toward the end of the speech, "is a settlement... a good understanding on all points with Russia."

In 1950 Churchill returned to this theme in a major foreign policy speech in Edinburgh on the eve of an election that would set the stage for his return to power the following year. Churchill hoped to find a "more exalted and august foundation for our safety than this grim and sombre balancing power of the [nuclear] bomb." It was in this speech that he first deployed the phrase "parley at the summit."

> Still I cannot help coming back to this idea of another talk with Soviet Russia upon the highest level. The idea appeals to me of a supreme effort to bridge the gulf between the two worlds so that each can live its life, if not in friendship, at least without the hatreds of the cold war. You must be careful to mark my words in these matters because I have not always been proved wrong. It is not easy to see how things could be worsened by a parley at the summit, if such a thing were possible.

While Churchill did not think "things could be worsened" by a summit, many other leaders on both sides of the Atlantic did. The Labour prime minister, Clement Attlee, thought the idea was merely a political gambit suggested by an electioneering Churchill. No doubt by proposing a "summit" to ease tensions Churchill hoped to deflect Labour's charge that he was a "warmonger." But in Washington, where the idea of a summit meeting was not colored by British politics, President Truman and Secretary of State Dean Acheson were politely skeptical in public and opposed in private.

Churchill's designs for a "parley at the summit" fell into abeyance with the outbreak of the Korean War. But the arrival of Dwight Eisenhower in the White House in 1953 and Stalin's death soon thereafter prompted Churchill to revive the idea of a summit—indeed it became the chief objective of his second premiership. He thought the death of Stalin presented a major opportunity for a diplomatic breakthrough with the USSR. Churchill's physician, Lord Moran, recorded in his diary, "The P.M. feels that Stalin's death may lead to a relaxation in tension. It is an opportunity that will not recur."

Eisenhower and his hawkish secretary of state, John Foster Dulles, were unenthusiastic about the idea. The president's chief of staff, Sherman Adams, recorded in his memoirs that "Eisenhower never felt that he would be able to negotiate successfully with Stalin." But even after Stalin's death, Eisenhower remained wary of a summit. He and Dulles worried that Churchill would be too conciliatory toward the Soviets, especially about the status of Germany. (The Soviet Union was not enthusiastic about a summit either; the Soviets distrusted Churchill as much as Ike and Dulles distrusted them.) Eisenhower and Dulles dragged their feet about pursuing an East-West summit and treated Churchill shabbily at a meeting in Bermuda where the prime minister and the president had gathered to discuss strategy. By the time the first East-West summit did take place, in Geneva in 1955, Churchill had retired from office, having handed the government over to Anthony Eden.

Not much came of that first summit; to the contrary, the supposed settlement of the Vietnam War that was part of the Geneva meeting quickly unraveled over the next few years. Nevertheless, it was followed by meetings between Kennedy and Khrushchev at Vienna in 1961; between Johnson and Kosygin at Glassboro, New Jersey, in 1966; between Nixon and Brezhnev at Moscow in 1972; between Ford and Brezhnev at Vladivostok in 1975; and between Carter and Brezhnev at Vienna. There were also the side-summits between American presidents and Chinese rulers which Nixon began in 1972. Some of these summits achieved diplomatic agreements on arms control and other small matters such as trade and cultural exchanges. Despite a brief period of détente in the 1970s, the Cold War and the arms race got worse.

Churchill, in the view of Klaus Larres, "became the first practitioner of détente in the post-war world."[1] And the historian John Lukacs has written that "perhaps a great chance may have been missed fifty years ago, when Churchill, as so often during his life, was willing to act on his own vision and go against the tide, and when he was right and his opponents were wrong."[2] It is impossible to know how history might have turned out had an early summit including Churchill taken place. He often overestimated the force of his own personality in face-to-face negotiations—a trait common to leading political figures. But the eventual course of diplomacy under Reagan and Gorbachev, which ended the Cold War, finally unfolded much as Churchill thought it might and at about the time he had predicted to John Colville in 1953. Yet, it was a bitter irony for Churchill that he, who coined the term "summit," never attended a Cold War summit conference.

CHAPTER 27

VINDICATED MISGIVINGS

THE UN WILL FAIL TO MEET EXPECTATIONS

One of Churchill's great disappointments of the interwar years was the failure of the League of Nations to fulfill its mission as a force for collective security, and he hoped its successor, the United Nations, would learn from the mistakes of the past. Looking back during World War II, Churchill concluded that the League had failed "because it was abandoned, and later on betrayed." But Churchill never let his idealism conquer his realism, and he was one of the first statesmen to declare plainly that the United Nations was a failure.

Churchill had supported the creation of the United Nations in the hope that it would prove more effective than the League of Nations. In 1943 he wrote to his foreign minister, Anthony Eden, "We hold strongly to a system of a League of Nations, which will include a Council of Europe, with an International Court and an armed power capable of enforcing its decisions." He was less certain that an effective global organization could be cobbled together quickly. President Roosevelt had originally hoped that a United Nations would emerge from the Yalta conference in 1945, but Churchill was skeptical: "I don't see any other way of realizing our hopes about a world organization in five or six days," he wrote to FDR. "Even the Almighty took seven."

He was correct. The final drafting of the UN Charter was put off to a special conference in San Francisco in May, by which time Roosevelt was dead. Looking forward to the San Francisco conference, Churchill wrote, "It will embody much of the structure and characteristics of its predecessor. All the work that was done in the past, all the experience that has been gathered by the working of the League of Nations, will not be cast away." But even as he was supportive, he sounded a wary note about the prospects for success: "We must labour that the World Organization, which the United Nations are creating at San Francisco, does not become an idle name, does not become a shield for the strong and a mockery for the weak."

Churchill had two concerns. The first was that the UN would try to solve too many world problems at the global rather than the regional level. He thought the UN should be an umbrella organization, with most conflicts mediated by regional organizations and "kicked upstairs" to the UN Security Council only when those regional bodies failed. His second concern was that the UN would succeed only so long as the major powers—the U.S., Britain, and the Soviet Union— worked in harmony. "What happens," Churchill asked in May 1946, "if the United Nations themselves are sundered by an awful schism, a clash of ideologies and passions? What is to happen if the United Nations give place, as they may do, to a vast confrontation of two parts of the world and two irreconcilably opposed conceptions of human society?"

By 1948 Churchill was already noting how the UN had been "reduced to a mere cockpit in which the representatives of mighty nations and ancient States hurl reproaches, taunts and recriminations at one another, to marshal public opinion and inflame the passions of their peoples in order to arouse and prepare them for when seems to be a remorselessly approaching third world war." The Cold War division of the world created the very deadlock that Churchill feared, with the notable exception of the Soviet boycott of the 1950 Security Council resolution that authorized UN intervention in the Korean War.

Despite these publicly expressed misgivings, Churchill also kept faith with the original vision of the UN throughout the late 1940s. In 1947 he said, "We accept, without question, the world supremacy of the United Nations organization," but the following year he observed that "it is still struggling for life and torn with dissension." Churchill praised the importance of the UN at length in his Iron Curtain speech in 1946, endorsing especially one feature that was and remains highly controversial with Americans—a UN armed force:

> The United Nations Organization must immediately begin
> to be equipped with an international armed force. In such
> a matter we can only go step by step, but we must begin
> now. I propose that each of the Powers and States should
> be invited to delegate a certain number of air squadrons to
> the service of the world organization.... [T]hey would be
> directed by the world organization.[1]

As late as 1950 Churchill still expressed hope that the UN could provide genuine collective security through its own armed forces: "We are all agreed that the only hope for the future of mankind lies in the creation of a strong effective world instrument, capable, at least, of maintaining peace and resisting aggression. I hope we shall pursue... the idea of a United Nations armed force."

Apart from American objections to an independent UN armed force under its own command, the Soviet veto ensured that UN-led collective security would seldom succeed. Early on, Churchill decried the Soviet "abuse" of its Security Council veto: "[I]t was never contemplated at any time that the veto should be used in the abrupt, arbitrary and almost continuous manner that we have seen it used."

Churchill reiterated his fears about the United Nations in 1947 in a speech in New York, where he was the guest of Henry Luce, the president of Time, Inc.

> The League of Nations made a far better start than the present UN, and the prospects for peace were brighter ten years after the first world war than they are now, only two-and-a-half years after the second war. But the lack of will-power and conscious purpose among the leading states and former allies drew us upon those slippery slopes of weak compromises, seeking the line of least resistance, which surely led to the abyss. The same thing is happening now with greater speed, and unless there is some moral renewal and conscious guidance of the good forces, while time remains, a prolonged eclipse of our civilization approaches.

Even then, Churchill offered public support for the UN, insisting, "We must not allow ourselves to be discouraged by the difficulties. Nor must we become impatient at the shortcomings of this United Nations conception in these early days."

But after the UN's repeated failure in the 1950s to fulfill its mission and the decline of the General Assembly, dominated by autocratic or non-democratic governments, into an anti-Western forum for Third World radicalism, Churchill concluded that the organization's inherent flaws—and not just the Soviet veto—guaranteed its failure. In a widely noted speech to the American Bar Association, meeting in London in 1957, Churchill declared,

I do not throw in my lot with those who say that Britain should leave the United Nations. However, it is certain that if the [General] Assembly continues to take its decisions on grounds of enmity, opportunism, or merely jealousy or petulance, the whole structure may be brought to nothing. The shape of the United Nations has changed greatly from its original form and from the intentions of its architects.... There are many cases where the United Nations have failed.

The end of the Cold War has not changed the United Nations. Russia, which inherited the Soviet Union's permanent seat on the Security Council, has continued to block effective collective security actions. Today, the "oil for food" scandal in Iraq, the brutality of UN observers in Africa, and the spectacle of tyrannical states entrusted with responsibility for human rights vindicate Churchill's prophecy of five decades ago.

CHAPTER 28

SUMMING UP

THE REMARKABLE CONSTANCY OF THE STATESMAN AND HIS FINAL PREDICTION

The title *Churchill: The Prophetic Statesman* may sound rather florid. Churchill himself might have dismissed it. Indeed, one of his jests about political life ridicules men who pose as biblical prophets warning a recalcitrant people. A politician, he said in 1902, needs "the ability to foretell what is going to happen tomorrow, next week, next month, and next year. And to have the ability afterwards to explain why it didn't happen." And Churchill, like any political figure with a long career, had his share of misfires. He reportedly once turned down a well-paying commission to write a magazine article on the topic "Will There Ever Be a Woman Prime Minister?" because he thought the idea was too outlandish even for his imaginative capacities. When he left 10 Downing Street in defeat after the 1945 election, Churchill told Anthony Eden that he did not expect he would ever return to the Cabinet Room: "I shall never sit in it again; you will, but I shall not." In 1932, shortly before Hitler took power, Churchill said, "I do not believe that we shall see another great war in our time,"—a puzzling departure from his repeated warnings about renewed European war because of the vindictiveness of the Versailles Treaty.

Of course, his momentary optimism about peace in Europe vanished immediately when the "new fact" of Hitler's arrival became apparent to him. Churchill often observed that "new facts" required statesmen to change their judgments. In the 1920s, when Churchill argued for reducing British defense spending, he dismissed the threat of Japan in the Far East, but the "new fact" of rising German militarism led him to say in 1936 that "should Germany at any time make war in Europe, we may be sure that Japan will immediately light a second conflagration in the Far East."

When I was a young man, Churchill told me that the key to statesmanship was to "study history, study history," and though he also said that he doubted strategic genius could be taught, one of his favorite maxims was "The longer you look back, the farther you can look forward." His historical sense was his anchor, and it accounted for his remarkable ability to see down the road amid dramatically changing circumstances. The philosopher Isaiah Berlin observed, "Far from changing his opinions too often, Churchill has scarcely, during a long and stormy career, altered them at all.... [T]he number of instances in which his views have in later years undergone any appreciable degree of change will be found astonishingly small."

Although his political and scientific predictions can be attributed to his historical imagination, some of his predictions defy easy explanation. Perhaps the most remarkable of these was his accurate prediction of the date of his own death. While shaving one morning in 1953, Churchill remarked to John Colville, "Today is the 24th of January. It's the day my father died. It's the day I shall die, too." He repeated this prediction to his son-in-law Christopher Soames shortly after his ninetieth birthday, in 1964. A few weeks later, on January 10, 1965, Churchill lapsed into a coma. Earlier that evening, during the nightly ritual of brandy and cigars, he had said to Soames, "It has been a grand journey, well worth making." He paused and added, "once." After he was stricken, the *Times* commented, "Life is clearly ebbing away, but how long it will be until the crossing of the bar it is impossible to say." Not for the first time the *Times* was wrong about Churchill. It *was* possible to say how long it would be—Churchill had already said it. Colville told the queen's private secretary, "He won't die until the 24th." Though Churchill seldom regained consciousness in the two weeks that followed, he survived to the predicted date. Churchill had survived his father by precisely three score and ten years—the full biblical lifetime—and had fulfilled many of his father's ambitions as well as his own.

Though Churchill's prescience cannot always be explained by his intellectual gifts or his romantic outlook, it is not satisfactory to attribute it to mysticism. One is drawn finally to the intangible but seemingly authentic reality of *destiny*. Churchill often understood himself as a man destined for great deeds, and his foresight in connecting his personal destiny to the tides of history is stupefying when taken as a whole.

Churchill's official biographer, Martin Gilbert, unearthed a remarkable fragment of an essay Churchill wrote at Harrow School in 1891, when he was barely sixteen years old:

> I can see vast changes coming over a new peaceful world; great upheavals, terrible struggles; wars such as one cannot imagine; and I tell you London will be in danger—London will be attacked and I shall be very prominent in the

defense of London. *I see further ahead than you do. I see
into the future.* This country will be subjected somehow, to
a tremendous invasion, by what means I do not know, but
I tell you I shall be in command of the defenses of London
and I will save London from disaster.... [D]reams of the
future are blurred but the main objective is clear. I repeat,
London will be in danger and in the high position I shall
occupy, it will fall to me to save the Capital and save the
Empire. [Emphasis added.]

It is difficult to read these remarkable words and to contemplate the
glorious career that followed without feeling chills down one's spine.
And even if some of Churchill's prophetic genius can be explained, it
is nevertheless difficult to comprehend, let along emulate fully. Those
who honor Sir Winston's memory and example might wish to take in
the words his daughter Mary wrote to him in 1951: "It is hardly in
the nature of things that your descendants should inherit your
genius—but I earnestly hope they may share in some ways the qualities of your heart."

ACKNOWLEDGMENTS

I f Winston Churchill was the "Man of the Century," Sir Martin Gilbert is the "Biographer of the Century." Any who write about Churchill are indebted to Gilbert's massive and comprehensive biography.

I thank Kay Halle for first suggesting a book of Churchill's prophecies. She was a friend of the Churchill family and the one principally responsible for the honorary citizenship awarded him in 1963.

I am also grateful to my friend, Winston Churchill II. I was his frequent guest at the House of Commons, and he visited me in Pueblo in 2003.

Jonathan Aitken, biographer of Nixon and great-nephew of Lord Beaverbrook, a member of Churchill's wartime cabinet, was an ever constant source of encouragement. Two other English friends are Lord

Cope, government whip under Margaret Thatcher, and Lord Cra-
thorne whose father served in Churchill's postwar cabinet.

Finally, I want to pay tribute to Regnery Publishing—to Alex
Novak who accepted the book as a Regnery History title; Maria Ruhl,
Managing Editor; Tom Spence, Editor; and Tess Civantos who labored
hard to work my book into shape.

NOTES

INTRODUCTION

1. Some military historians dispute this frequent claim, pointing out that the British army engaged in cavalry charges in the Boer War just a few years later.

2. Winston Churchill, *The River War*, unabridged (1899), chapter 19.

3. Violet Bonham Carter, *Winston Churchill: An Intimate Portrait*, p. 25.

4. William Manchester, *The Last Lion: Winston Spencer Churchill: Visions of Glory, 1874–1932*, vol. 1 (Little, Brown and Company, 1983), p. 12.

5. Isaiah Berlin, "Winston Churchill in 1940," *Personal Impressions* (London: Hogarth Press, 1981), p. 4.

6. Peter Stansky, *Churchill: A Profile*, p., 197, in Manchester, *The Last Lion*, vol. 1, p. 12.

7. Winston Churchill, *My Early Life* (1930), p. 67.

CHAPTER 1

1. Winston Churchill, *The World Crisis* (New York: Charles Scribner's Sons, 1931; republished New York: The Free Press, 2005), p. 3. The three previous occasions on which "the British people [had] rescued Europe from a military domination" were the wars of Philip II of Spain, the wars of Louis XIV of France, and the upheavals from the French Revolution through the Napoleonic wars.

CHAPTER 2

1. Speech at Guildhall, Plymouth, August 17, 1900, in Winston Churchill, *The World Crisis* (New York: Charles Scribner's Sons, 1931; republished New York: The Free Press, 2005).
2. William Manchester, *The Last Lion: Winston Spencer Churchill: Visions of Glory, 1874–1932*, vol. 1 (Little, Brown and Company, 1983), pp. 318–19.
3. Churchill, *The World Crisis*, p. 3.

CHAPTER 3

1. Randolph Churchill, *Winston S. Churchill*, vol. 2, "Young Statesman, 1901–1914," p. 500.

CHAPTER 9

1. Martin Gilbert, *Churchill: A Life* (Henry Holt and Company, LLC, 1991), p. xix.
2. In Paul Johnson, *Churchill* (Penguin Books, 2010), p. 23.

CHAPTER 14

1. James C. Humes, *The Wit & Wisdom of Winston Churchill* (HarperCollins, 1994), p. 155.

CHAPTER 17

1. John Strawson, *Churchill and Hitler* (Constable, 1997), p. 182.
2. John Lukacs, *Churchill: Visionary, Statesman, Historian* (Yale University Press, 2004), p. 5.
3. William Manchester, *The Last Lion: Winston Spencer Churchill: Alone, 1932–40*, vol. 2 (Little, Brown and Company, 1983), p. 82.
4. Ibid., p. 311.
5. Ibid., pp. 82–83.

CHAPTER 22

1. Martin Gilbert, *Winston S. Churchill: Never Despair*, 1874–1965, vol. 8 (Stoddart Kids, 1988), p. 7.

CHAPTER 23

1. Speech to the House of Commons, March 1, 1955.

CHAPTER 24

1. Martin Gilbert, *Winston S. Churchill: Never Despair*, 1874–1965, vol. 8 (Stoddart Kids, 1988), p. 684.

CHAPTER 25

1. Martin Gilbert, *Winston S. Churchill: Never Despair*, 1874–1965, vol. 8 (Stoddart Kids, 1988), p. 680.

CHAPTER 26

1. Klaus Larres, *Churchill's Cold War: The Politics of Personal Diplomacy* (New Haven: Yale University Press, 2002), p. xv.
2. John Lukacs, "Blood, Sweat, and Fears," *The New Republic*, January 13, 2003, p. 37.

CHAPTER 27

1. Scholarly opinion is nearly unanimous that delegating American armed forces to UN command, as Churchill suggested, would be unconstitutional.

INDEX